Connecticut Legal Research

Carolina Academic Press
Legal Research Series

Tenielle Fordyce-Ruff, Series Editor
Suzanne E. Rowe, Series Editor Emerita

Arizona, Fourth Edition — Tamara S. Herrera
Arkansas, Second Edition — Coleen M. Barger, Cheryl L. Reinhart & Cathy L. Underwood
California, Fourth Edition — Aimee Dudovitz, Sarah Laubach & Suzanne E. Rowe
Colorado, Second Edition — Robert Michael Linz
Connecticut, Second Edition — Anne Rajotte & Jessica Rubin
Federal, Second Edition — Mary Garvey Algero, Spencer L. Simons, Suzanne E. Rowe, Scott Childs & Sarah E. Ricks
Florida, Fifth Edition — Barbara J. Busharis, Anne E. Mullins & Suzanne E. Rowe
Georgia, Second Edition — Margaret Butler & Thomas Striepe
Hawai'i — Victoria Szymczak, Cory Lenz & Roberta Woods
Idaho, Third Edition — Tenielle Fordyce-Ruff
Illinois, Second Edition — Mark E. Wojcik
Indiana — Ashley Ames Ahlbrand & Michelle Trumbo
Iowa, Third Edition — John D. Edwards, Karen L. Wallace & Melissa H. Weresh
Kansas — Joseph A. Custer & Christopher L. Steadham
Kentucky, Second Edition — William A. Hilyerd, Kurt X. Metzmeier & David J. Ensign
Louisiana, Fourth Edition — Mary Garvey Algero
Massachusetts, Second Edition — E. Joan Blum & Shaun B. Spencer
Michigan, Fourth Edition — Cristina D. Lockwood
Minnesota — Suzanne Thorpe
Mississippi — Kristy L. Gilliland
Missouri, Fourth Edition — Wanda M. Temm & Julie M. Cheslik
New York, Fourth Edition — Elizabeth G. Adelman, Courtney L. Selby, Brian Detweiler & Kathleen Darvil
North Carolina, Third Edition — Brenda D. Gibson, Julie L. Kimbrough, Laura P. Graham & Nichelle J. Perry
North Dakota — Anne E. Mullins & Tammy Pettinato Oltz
Ohio, Second Edition — Sara Sampson, Katherine L. Hall & Carolyn Broering-Jacobs
Oklahoma — Darin K. Fox, Darla W. Jackson & Courtney L. Selby
Oregon, Fifth Edition — Suzanne E. Rowe & Megan Austin
Pennsylvania, Second Edition — Barbara J. Busharis, Catherine M. Dunn, Bonny L. Tavares & Carla P. Wale
Tennessee, Second Edition — Scott Childs, Sibyl Marshall & Carol McCrehan Parker
Texas, Second Edition — Spencer L. Simons
Washington, Second Edition — Julie A. Heintz-Cho, Tom Cobb & Mary A. Hotchkiss
West Virginia, Second Edition — Hollee Schwartz Temple
Wisconsin — Patricia Cervenka & Leslie Behroozi
Wyoming, Second Edition — Debora A. Person & Tawnya K. Plumb

Connecticut Legal Research

Second Edition

Anne Rajotte
Jessica Rubin

Tenielle Fordyce-Ruff, Series Editor
Suzanne E. Rowe, Series Editor Emerita

Carolina Academic Press
Durham, North Carolina

Library of Congress Cataloging-in-Publication Data

Names: Rajotte, Anne, author. | Rubin, Jessica, author.
Title: Connecticut legal research / by Anne Rajotte, Jessica Rubin.
Description: Second edition. | Durham, North Carolina : Carolina Academic Press, LLC, [2022] | Series: Legal research series | Includes index.
Identifiers: LCCN 2022008923 | ISBN 9781531023171 (paperback) | ISBN 9781531023188 (ebook)
Subjects: LCSH: Legal research—Connecticut.
Classification: LCC KFC3675 .H96 2022 | DDC 340.072/0746—dc23/eng/20220502
LC record available at https://lccn.loc.gov/2022008923

Carolina Academic Press
700 Kent Street
Durham, North Carolina 27701
(919) 489-7486
www.cap-press.com

Printed in the United States of America.

Summary of Contents

Contents

List of Tables

Preface and Acknowledgments

This is a book for Connecticut students and lawyers; it is intended for law students, paralegals, and practitioners who need to research Connecticut resources, and anyone else seeking an understanding of Connecticut legal authorities.

In creating this text, we aimed to develop a practical resource to explain sources of Connecticut law and the process of researching legal issues in Connecticut, supplemented with information regarding legal research in the federal system. We included tables to illustrate search strategies and complicated conceptual issues in order to help the reader visualize and better understand the material. We also included a chapter on legal writing to demonstrate the intersection between the process of research and writing. Finally, throughout our explanations of research strategies, we emphasized cost-effective research approaches so that a researcher can conserve time and client resources.

We express our deep gratitude to Marla Katz, research assistant and editor-in-chief of the Connecticut Law Review. Drawing on her expertise as a former writing consultant and graduate assistant of the St. John's University Writing Center and her perspective as a law student, Marla greatly improved the text. She contributed artistic talent to develop the text's tables and used her experience as a student law review editor to perfect the chapter on citations. Alexandra Bostick provided substantial assistance with editing and creating tables. We are also grateful for the support of UConn Law School, specifically Dean Eboni Nelson, Associate Dean for Faculty Development and Intellectual Life Richard Wilson, and Director of the Law Library Jessica de Perio Wittman, who supported our work. Additionally, Tenielle Fordyce-Ruff, the series editor, provided valuable advice and edits, and provided us with the tremendous opportunity to work on a new edition of *Connecticut Legal Research*. Special thanks to Suzanne Rowe for her vision and leadership in creating this state-specific research series.

Lastly, we acknowledge and thank our UConn Law School students who have, over many years of shared office and classroom conversations, sharpened our explanations and teaching through their questions and puzzled expressions. They taught us which topics warranted careful and deep explanations. Our students' interests and needs drove the content of this edition, and we hope that readers find this book especially useful as a result.

Finally, writing this text in 2021, during the COVID pandemic and associated remote teaching and learning, we carefully considered how legal practice and legal research will evolve in the near future. We strove to create a text that would work equally well for in-person research and remote research, and we hope that this edition will therefore stand the test of time.

Anne Rajotte and Jessica Rubin

Series Note

The Legal Research Series published by Carolina Academic Press includes an increasing number of titles from states around the country. The goal of each book is to provide law students, practitioners, paralegals, college students, and laypeople with the essential elements of legal research in each state. Unlike more bibliographic texts, the Legal Research Series books seek to explain concisely both the sources of state law research and the process for conducting legal research effectively.

Connecticut Legal Research

Chapter 1

Foundations of Legal Research and Analysis

Lawyers, paralegals, and law students have one thing in common—they need to be effective and efficient legal researchers. Legal research requires these individuals to identify, understand, synthesize, and apply legal sources to answer questions or resolve problems. Effective legal research generates sources that provide the bases for convincing persuasive arguments, objective predictive analyses, strategic business transactions, and more. In all cases, providing legal advice and implementing client decisions are based on the results of legal research. Consequently, legal research must be efficient, current, accurate, and comprehensive.

I. Introduction to Legal Research

Legal research is an essential lawyering skill. It is the process through which members of the legal profession systematically locate and analyze information from various sources to help them answer questions or resolve problems. In practice, legal research allows lawyers to discover rules, prior decisions, and interpretations to understand and predict the outcomes of their current matters. Legal research, therefore, equips lawyers with information to counsel clients, advocate to courts, and advance positions.

This book provides instruction on the resources and analyses required for effective legal research in Connecticut. This book explains how to conduct legal research through print and online sources, and it explains how to select the most efficient, current, and accurate sources for legal research.

A. Importance of Legal Research

Legal research is a skill that is critical to law students' and lawyers' successes. Thorough legal research allows law students and lawyers to serve their clients through careful inquiries into relevant authorities and other information that may assist in solving clients' problems. It also results in strong stewardship of clients' resources.

Rule 1.1 of the Model Rules of Professional Conduct, the American Bar Association's model rules for legal professionals, requires lawyers to provide competent client representation, which includes reasonably necessary legal knowledge, skill, thoroughness, and preparation.[1] Comments 1, 2, and 5 to Rule 1.1 contemplate that competence depends, in part, on research skills—determining what kinds of legal problems a situation may involve and analyzing the factual and legal elements of the problem.[2]

For members of the legal profession, a basic principle of legal research is that it requires "a logical, methodological approach with attention to detail."[3] However, most law students and professionals have not mastered the basic principle, let alone the intensive process of legal research. A 2015 survey among three hundred hiring partners and senior associates supervising new associates showed that new associates tend to lack advanced skills in legal research, despite spending 40 to 60 percent of their time conducting legal research.[4] The survey suggested that legal research competency is requisite for success in practice, especially because employers increasingly seek advanced skills in legal research from new associates.[5] Developing advanced skills will benefit law students preparing to enter practice and lawyers in practice, as the skills will allow them to better complete assignments, counsel clients, and strategize throughout their careers.

B. Challenges of Legal Research

Legal research is complex, challenging, and often extremely time-consuming. In the United States, the law derives from various sources and different jurisdictions, and it constantly evolves through new judicial opinions, statutes, regulations, agency interpretations, and scholarship. As a result, a researcher must consult various sources and update their results in an

1. Model Rules of Pro. Conduct r. 1.1 (Am. Bar Ass'n 2020).

2. *Id.*, r. 1.1, cmts. 1, 2, 5.

3. Kurt Meyer, *Teaching Legal Research to Today's Digital Natives*, 21 AALL Spectrum 12, 14 (2017).

4. LexisNexis, *Hiring Partners Reveal New Attorney Readiness for Real World Practice* 3 (2015), https://www.lexisnexis.com/documents/pdf/20150325064926_large.pdf.

5. *Id.* at 1.

appropriate, timely manner. In addition, legal research often proceeds in a nonlinear manner. A researcher must be flexible and willing to adopt new approaches. Finally, some legal sources cost money to acquire or access. Because of these demands, legal research is often time-consuming and expensive for clients, and a researcher should strive for cost-effective, efficient methods.

C. Legal Research and Legal Analysis

Legal research and legal analysis are interwoven. Consequently, this book incorporates legal research and legal analysis in its explanation of best research practices. For example, in conducting research, a researcher must appreciate the function, scope, perspective, relative importance, and binding nature of each source that they consult. In addition, they must understand the key facts and legal elements that will be relevant in answering a question or solving a problem. Therefore, a researcher should never consider legal research to be a process separate from legal analysis.

II. The U.S. Legal System

The U.S. legal system is a common law system in which the law derives from a combination of enacted law and, where no enacted law directly applies, case law. Enacted law includes federal and state constitutions, statutes, and regulations. Case law derives from judicial opinions issued by federal and state courts.

At the state level, legislatures often codify common law from their courts in order to give the permanence of a statute, to modify a rule, or to replace a case's outcome with legislation. Most common law is found at the state level. However, there is a limited body of federal common law, which consists of rules made and applied by federal courts absent a controlling federal statute.[6]

A. Federalism

The United States follows a system of federalism, meaning that the federal and state governments and their respective legal systems coexist. The federal

---

6. *Common Law*, Legal Information Institute, https://www.law.cornell.edu/wex/common_law (last visited May 27, 2021).

and state governments are somewhat autonomous. However, under the U.S. Constitution's doctrine of dual sovereignty, the state governments have surrendered some powers to the federal government, while retaining other powers, such as the power to enact laws.[7] As a result, a legal matter may be governed by federal law, state law, or both. A researcher must consider which authority applies. This book assumes that the legal matter to be researched is governed by Connecticut law, but it also indicates where federal law applies.

B. Branches of Government

Within each jurisdiction—the United States and Connecticut—there are three branches of government. At the federal level, the executive branch includes the president; vice president; cabinet; and executive branch agencies, departments, and other groups. While the power of the executive branch is vested in the president, all members of the executive branch enforce federal laws.[8] The legislative branch includes Congress—the Senate and the House of Representatives—and the agencies that provide support to Congress. The legislative branch has the sole power to enact legislation.[9] The judicial branch consists of the U.S. Supreme Court and other federal courts. The federal judiciary has the sole power to interpret the law, determine its constitutionality, and apply it to cases.[10]

---

7. *Federalism*, Legal Information Institute, https://www.law.cornell.edu/wex/federalism (last visited May 27, 2021).

8. *Branches of the U.S. Government*, USA.gov (Jan. 21, 2021), https://www.usa.gov/branches-of-government. *See also The Executive Branch*, The White House, https://www.whitehouse.gov/about-the-white-house/our-government/the-executive-branch/ (last visited May 27, 2021).

9. *Branches of the U.S. Government*, *supra*. *See also The Legislative Branch*, The White House, https://www.whitehouse.gov/about-the-white-house/our-government/the-legislative-branch/ (last visited May 27, 2021).

10. *Branches of the U.S. Government*, *supra*. *See also The Judicial Branch*, The White House, https://www.whitehouse.gov/about-the-white-house/our-government/the-judicial-branch/ (last visited May 27, 2021).

At the state level in Connecticut, the executive branch includes the governor, lieutenant governor, secretary of state, treasurer, comptroller, and attorney general. The executive branch enforces the laws of the state.[11] The legislative branch includes the General Assembly, which consists of the Senate and the House of Representatives. Currently, there are thirty-six state senators and 151 state representatives, representing districts based on population. The state senators and state representatives establish state legislation.[12] Finally, the judicial branch includes those sitting on Connecticut's superior, appellate, and supreme courts. Judges interpret the law and apply it to cases in a manner that ensures the just resolution of legal issues in the state.[13] Table 1-1 depicts the structure of the Connecticut and U.S. government.

Table 1-1. Structure of U.S. and Connecticut Governments

<table>
<tr><th colspan="6">Branches of Government</th></tr>
<tr><th colspan="2">Executive Branch</th><th colspan="2">Legislative Branch</th><th colspan="2">Judicial Branch</th></tr>
<tr><th>Federal</th><th>State of Connecticut</th><th>Federal</th><th>State of Connecticut</th><th>Federal</th><th>State of Connecticut</th></tr>
<tr><td>President
Vice President
Cabinet
Federal Agencies, Departments and Other Groups</td><td>Governor
Lieutenant Governor
Secretary of State
Treasurer
Comptroller
Attorney General</td><td>Congress
(Senate and House of Representatives)
Federal Agencies</td><td>General Assembly
(State Senate and State House of Representatives)</td><td>U.S. Supreme Court
U.S. Court of Appeals
U.S. District Courts</td><td>Supreme Court
Appellate Court
Superior Courts</td></tr>
</table>

11. *Government*, CT.gov, https://portal.ct.gov/About/Government (last visited May 27, 2021).

12. *Id.*

13. *Id.*

III. Sources of Law

Laws can be classified by their source and by their binding force on subsequent matters.

A. Primary Sources of Law

Primary authorities are laws produced by government bodies with law-making power. Each branch of government produces its own type of law. Within the executive branch, the chief executive issues treaties and orders, and agencies write rules and regulations; within the legislative branch, Congress writes statutes; within the judicial branch, courts write judicial opinions. Because these three branches exist in the U.S. and the Connecticut governments, they produce the four primary sources of law for each jurisdiction. Table 1-2 depicts primary sources of law in the Connecticut and U.S. legal systems.

Table 1-2. Primary Sources of Federal and State Law

Primary Sources of Law							
Constitutions		Statutes		Regulations		Judicial Opinions	
Federal	State	Federal	State	Federal	State	Federal	State
United States Consti-tution	State Consti-tutions	U.S.C. U.S.C.A. U.S.C.S.	State Editions	*Federal Register* C.F.R.	State Editions of *Federal Register*	U.S. S. Ct. L. Ed. F F.2d F.3d F.Supp F. Supp. 2d F. Supp. 3d	State Reporters

Chapters 4, 6, 7, and 12 explain primary sources of law in more detail, but the most common primary sources are introduced below.

1. Constitutions

The United States is governed by the U.S. Constitution and individual state constitutions. The U.S. Constitution, drafted in 1787 by the original thirteen colonies, "reform[ed] and restructure[d] the national government and establish[ed] the relationship between the federal government and the states collectively and the relationships between the individual states."[14] The U.S. Constitution often serves as a model for individual state constitutions. Each state has a state constitution, ratified by its citizens in order to provide the fundamental principles from which all other law derives. For example, the previous Constitution of Connecticut was submitted to its people in 1818. It received 13,918 votes in favor of its ratification and 12,364 votes against its ratification. Following the vote, the governor issued a proclamation that the Constitution of Connecticut was to be observed as supreme law of the state.[15]

Constitutions are published in the same manner as statutes.[16] The U.S. Constitution is published in three editions of the *United States Code: United States Code* (U.S.C.); *United States Code Annotated* (U.S.C.A.) (Westlaw); and *United States Code Service* (U.S.C.S.) (Lexis). Individual state constitutions are usually published in compilations of state statutes.

It is important to note that the U.S. Constitution and individual state constitutions are considered primary authority because they issue directly from federal and state law-making bodies.

2. Statutes

Statutes are laws enacted by legislative bodies at the federal and state levels. Some statutes are enacted exclusively at the federal level by Congress, while others are enacted exclusively at the state level by state legislatures.

Federal statutes are published in three intervals as slip laws, session laws, and codes. First, a statute is published as a slip law, in print or online, soon after it is enacted. A slip law provides information about its enactment date, location of codification, and legislative history. A slip law may be cited by a public law number, which includes the number of the legislative session and the number of the bill in that session. Second, a statute is published as a session law, which includes all the slip laws enacted in a legislative session

---

14. United States Constitution, *Black's Law Dictionary* (5th pocket ed., Thomson West 2016).

15. Conn. Const. of 1818.

16. *See* discussion *infra* section III.A.2.

arranged chronologically by enactment date. Because a session law contains the complete text of statutes as enacted, it is the controlling form of the law. That is, a session law controls if there is a difference between it and a code. Third, a statute is published as a code, which incorporates related statutes and amendments into the text of the existing statute. A code is arranged by individual subjects or "titles."

Federal statutes appear in three editions of the *United States Code: United States Code* (U.S.C.); *United States Code Annotated* (U.S.C.A.) (Westlaw); and *United States Code Service* (U.S.C.S.) (Lexis). The U.S.C. only contains the text of the statute. The U.S.C.A. and U.S.C.S. contain the text of the statute, as well as references to other primary and secondary sources.

Most state statutes are published in a manner similar to federal statutes. For example, most states publish their statutes as slip laws, then have official publications of their session laws. Also similar to federal statutes, state statutes tend to appear in different editions.[17]

3. Regulations

Regulations are rules or orders, with legal force, that are issued by administrative agencies of the executive branches of the federal and state governments.[18] A regulation is issued pursuant to a statutory authority. In other words, a statute must be enacted that directs an administrative agency to issue a regulation.

Though regulations are primary sources of law, they are not equal in weight to federal or state constitutions, statutes, or cases. A regulation may be overridden by a constitution or a statute. Alternatively, a regulation may be overruled by a court, if it holds that an administrative agency did not have the authority to issue the regulation,[19] or by Congress under the Congressional Review Act.[20]

---

17. For more information on statutes, see Mindy Kent, *Statutes: US and State Codes*, Harvard Law School Library, https://guides.library.harvard.edu/law/statutes #s-lg-page-section-2072055 (last updated May 5, 2021).

18. Regulation, *Black's Law Dictionary* (5th pocket ed., Thomson West 2016).

19. *Basics of Legal Research: Primary Sources*, The Law Library of Louisiana, https://lasc.libguides.com/c.php?g=436789&p=2980672 (last updated May 19, 2021).

20. Maeve P. Carey & Christopher M. Davis, *The Congressional Review Act (CRA): Frequently Asked Questions*, Cong. Rsch. Serv., R43992, (2020).

Federal regulations are printed in the *Federal Register*, which is published five days per week by the U.S. Government Printing Office. Regulations are then published by subject matter in the *Code of Federal Regulations* (C.F.R.). State regulations are often published in a state version of the *Federal Register* and then codified by subject matter.[21]

4. Judicial Opinions

The judicial branch of the United States and the judicial branch of Connecticut each have three levels of courts—trial, appellate, and supreme. Within the federal jurisdiction of the United States, there are ninety-four trial courts, or courts of original jurisdiction, that are called U.S. district courts; thirteen appellate courts, or courts of intermediate appeals, that are called U.S. courts of appeals; and one Supreme Court.[22] Table 1-3 depicts the structure of the federal and state judiciaries. Within the state of Connecticut, the trial courts are called superior courts, and there is an appellate court and a supreme court. The superior court system includes thirteen judicial districts, twenty geographical areas, and twelve juvenile districts. It has four principal trial divisions—civil, criminal, housing, and family—that have topical jurisdiction to hear specific matters. Most litigation occurs in the superior court system. In addition, Connecticut has a separate probate court system including fifty-four probate court districts and six regional children's probate courts. Probate court matters may be appealed to the appropriate superior court.[23] Table 1-4 depicts the structure of the federal courts, and Table 1-5 depicts the structure of the state of Connecticut courts.

---

21. John C. Dernbach et al., *A Practical Guide to Legal Writing and Legal Method* 17 (7th ed., Wolters Kluwer 2021).

22. *Court Role and Structure*, United States Courts, https://www.uscourts.gov/about-federal-courts/court-role-and-structure (last visited May 28, 2021).

23. *About Connecticut Courts*, State of Connecticut Judicial Branch, https://www.jud.ct.gov/ystday/orgcourt.html (last visited May 28, 2021) (detailing the organization of Connecticut courts).

Table 1-3. Structure of Federal and State Court Systems

Structure of the Court System					
Trial Level		Appellate Level		Supreme Level	
Federal	State of Connecticut	Federal	State of Connecticut	Federal	State of Connecticut
U.S. District Courts (94)	Connecticut Superior Court	U.S. Court of Appeals (13)	Connecticut Appellate Court (1)	U.S. Supreme Court (1)	Connecticut Supreme Court (1)
	Connecticut Probate Court				

Table 1-4. Structure of Federal Court System

Structure of the Federal Court System					
U.S. Supreme Court *Court of Final Appeals*					
U.S. Courts of Appeals *Courts of Intermediate Appeals*			U.S. Court of Appeals for the Federal Circuit *Court of Intermediate Appeals*		
U.S. District Courts Courts of Original Jurisdiction	U.S. Bankruptcy Courts Courts of Original Jurisdiction	U.S. Tax Court Court of Original Jurisdiction	U.S. District Court Court of Original Jurisdiction	U.S. Court of International Trade Court of Original Jurisdiction	U.S. Court of Federal Claims Court of Original Jurisdiction

Table 1-5. Structure of Connecticut Court System

Structure of the State of Connecticut Court System
Connecticut Supreme Court *Court of Final Appeals*
Connecticut Appellate Court *Court of Intermediate Appeals*
Connecticut Superior Courts *Courts of Original Jurisdiction*
Connecticut Probate Courts* *Courts of Original Jurisdiction* **A Probate Court matter may be appealed to the appropriate Superior Court*

The courts of the United States and Connecticut are all critical to serving the interests of justice, though the courts have different functions. The federal and state trial courts have the unique role of reviewing evidence and testimony to determine the facts of a case and applying the law to those facts. Appellate and supreme courts do not review the facts of a case; instead, they review the application of the law to determine whether the lower court made an error in that application.

A court's jurisdiction and level are essential to determining the impact of any given decision on subsequent cases and research questions. Specifically, a researcher must always determine whether a judicial opinion is mandatory or persuasive precedent—meaning, respectively, that the judicial opinion is binding upon the court or that it is not binding upon the court and therefore need not be followed.

Judicial opinions are published in hardbound volumes with pamphlet supplements that contain opinions that are too recent to be published in hardbound. Decisions by the U.S. Supreme Court are published in *United States Reports* (U.S.), the official version; the *Supreme Court Reporter* (S. Ct.); and *United States Supreme Court Reports, Lawyers' Edition* (L. Ed.). Decisions by federal appeals courts are published in *Federal Reporter* (F., F.2d, F.3d), and decisions by federal district courts are published in *Federal Supplement* (F. Supp., F. Supp. 2d, F. Supp. 3d). However, not all decisions by federal appeals courts and federal district courts are published. Alternatively, most states publish their own judicial opinions.[24]

B. Precedent

In a common law system, a large portion of the law comes from judicial opinions or *precedent*. An important step in legal research and legal analysis is determining if precedent is mandatory or persuasive.

For precedent to be mandatory, or binding on a subsequent case, two requirements must be met. First, the precedent must be sufficiently similar to the subsequent case in its important facts and reasoning. Second, the precedent must come from a court within the same jurisdiction and at a higher level than the court deciding the current case. Where both requirements are met, a court will follow the doctrine of *stare decisis* and follow the precedent of similar cases from higher courts in the jurisdiction.

C. Mandatory Authority vs. Persuasive Authority

Mandatory authority is law that binds the court deciding a subsequently litigated case. On a question of Connecticut law, mandatory authority includes—in descending order—Constitution of Connecticut, statutes, regulations, administrative/court rules, and decisions of Connecticut courts at a level higher than the court deciding the given case.

Persuasive authority is law that does not bind the court, but it might influence the court's decision. Persuasive authority derives from a court that is lower than or at the same level as the court deciding the given case; from a court in a different jurisdiction; or from secondary sources of law.[25]

A researcher's goal is to find any mandatory authority that will answer the research questions. Where mandatory authority does not exist, persuasive authority may be used to advocate for an outcome.

---

24. Dernbach et al., *supra*, at 19.

25. For more information on secondary sources of law, see discussion *infra* section III.D.

D. Secondary Sources of Law

Secondary sources of law are materials that are written about the law to help locate, analyze, or update primary sources of law. Because they are not law, secondary sources always constitute persuasive authority; they never constitute mandatory authority. Chapter 3 explains secondary sources in more detail, but the most common secondary sources are introduced below.

1. Legal Encyclopedias

Legal encyclopedias provide a general overview of the law on a wide variety of topics. They also provide references to primary authorities, functioning as explanatory sources and research aids. Legal encyclopedias are organized by subject matter and suborganized according to alphabetical order. There are two national legal encyclopedias—*Corpus Juris Secundum* (C.J.S.) and *American Jurisprudence*, second edition (Am. Jur. 2d). Some states have their own legal encyclopedias, but Connecticut does not.

2. American Law Reports

American Law Reports (ALR) contain lengthy articles and extensive research aids. The articles tend to be from a practitioner's view, to focus on narrow topics, and to survey the law in different jurisdictions. While a researcher is not guaranteed to find an ALR article on a topic, locating one is beneficial because it will provide a thorough explanation and citations to primary authorities.

3. Legal Periodicals

Law reviews and law journals publish scholarly articles that explore specific legal issues in great depth. These articles often provide an explanation of an area of law before advancing the author's thesis. Law students, practitioners, professors, and judges can write these articles.

Each state's bar journal contains articles of interest to practitioners in that state. The Connecticut Bar Association publishes the *Connecticut Bar Journal*. The American Bar Association publishes the *ABA Journal*.

4. Treatises, Practice Guides, and Other Books

Legal texts can provide in-depth discussions of legal subject matter and references to primary authorities. Legal texts include treatises, practice books, hornbooks, and Nutshells. They explain particular areas of law and vary in their depth of coverage.

5. *Digests*

Digests are topical indexes, alphabetically organized, that collect and summarize judicial opinions on specific points of law. Digests allow researchers to easily move from a digest summary to a judicial opinion.

6. *Restatements*

Restatements provide summaries of the law in particular areas, as well as commentary on the law and recommended changes. Restatements are typically written by legal scholars and have the potential to become primary law, if adopted by a state's legislature.

7. *Looseleaf Services*

Looseleaf services are sources that gather and present primary and secondary authorities under one title. In areas like tax, bankruptcy, and environmental law, a single looseleaf service may contain statutes, administrative regulations, case annotations, agency opinions, and commentary by scholars and practitioners.

8. *Practice Materials*

Practice materials typically explain the law and related procedure, and include tools such as model forms, checklists, toolkits, and model language for contracts and agreements.

9. *Citators*

Citators provide legal researchers with a method for locating a case and learning how courts treated it in subsequent cases. Essentially, citators inform researchers how courts have referred to the judiciary in subsequent cases. Have later courts followed the given precedent? Questioned it? Distinguished subsequent cases from it? These leads to later courts' treatment of a given case can be valuable in testing the validity of an opinion and in finding additional, related opinions.

IV. Organization of This Book

This book serves as a manual for the research process. It explains how to plan research, how to conduct research through various sources, and how to use research results to answer questions and explain analyses.

Chapter 2 provides a guide to factual analysis and planning research. In addition, it explains how to be strategic, effective, and efficient in the research process. Chapter 3 explains how to use secondary sources of law, as they provide a strong analytical starting point and will lead to primary sources.

Chapters 4, 5, 6, and 12 explain how to locate and analyze various primary sources including constitutions, statutes, regulations, legislative history materials, administrative agency decisions, and court rules.

Chapters 7, 8, 9, and 10 discuss how to locate, reference, understand, and update judicial opinions in legal writing.

Chapter 11 suggests methods for communicating research results in well-organized predictive and persuasive legal writing.

Finally—because Connecticut is a global insurance capital and, as such, is home to many national and international insurers—chapter 13 demonstrates how to conduct research on matters of insurance law.

Chapter 2

The Legal Research Process

I. The Stages of the Legal Research Process

Legal research is the systematic search for information in order to examine legal issues, answer legal questions, and inform client decisions. The legal research process begins when a researcher realizes a need for legal information. This may come in the form of a client's problem, an assignment from a supervisor, or many other scenarios. The first steps in the legal research process include defining the problem, assessing the available resources, choosing appropriate resources, and extracting information from those resources. The second step involves organizing and synthesizing the information located into a research product. The third step, which is especially important, is to update the information, thus validating its currency. The final step is to communicate the research results through a report, memorandum, brief, or letter, depending on the audience.

A. Research Planning

Research planning is essential to conducting effective, efficient, and thorough research. Creating a plan ensures that the research will begin with an analysis of the research question, a roadmap of sources to be consulted, and an initial list of terms for browsing and searching. Investing a small amount of time in research planning at the outset of the process prevents wasting time conducting aimless research or retracing steps.

1. Problem Analysis

The first step in the research process is to define the research problem and identify the information that is needed to address it. This requires the researcher to determine the legally relevant facts, then formulate the specific questions to be answered in order to complete an assignment, advise a client, or accomplish another task.

There are several techniques for analyzing a problem in preparation for legal research, but the general goal of all the techniques is to identify the legally relevant facts related to the problem. Doing so will allow the researcher to account for the parties involved, nonparties involved, proper jurisdiction, claims, and remedies. Table 2-1 depicts several common techniques for analyzing a problem.

Table 2-1. Common Techniques for Analyzing a Problem

TARP	5Ws	TAPP
Things-What are the relevant objects involved? Actions-What did those involved do or not do? Relief Sought-What are the parties entitled to? Parties-Who is involved?	Who-Who is involved? What-What was involved in the incident(s)? When-When did the incident(s) happen? Where-Where did the incident(s) take place? Why-Why did things happen the way they did?	Things-What are the relevant objects involved? Actions-What did those involved do or not do? People-Who is involved? Places-Where did the incident(s) take place?

The second step is to use the factual analysis to identify the legal issues to be researched. The researcher should categorize the facts with descriptive terms, categorizing broadly then more specifically, until the legal issues arising from the facts are articulated. Then the researcher should categorize the resulting legal issues into areas of law, which will assist in the selection of appropriate secondary sources. Table 2-2 depicts a TARP analysis.

Table 2-2. TARP Analysis

Facts	A software engineer signed an agreement with her employer when hired that she would not take a job with any company that creates any software within 100 miles for three years. She has been offered a job in a city fifty miles away at a company that makes software but does not compete directly with her current employer and would like to take the job.
TARP Analysis	Things: non-compete agreement Actions: employee agreed not to work for other companies that produce software within a time and geographic limit Relieft Sought: to determine if the contract allows her to take the job Parties: employer and employee
Legal Issues	Does the agreement allow the employee to take the job she has been offered? If not, is the agreement enforceable?
Areas of Law	Contract Law Employment Law

Finally, informed by both the factual and legal analyses, the researcher should consider which subjects and terms may be associated with the research questions. These subjects and terms may be used to locate, browse, and search legal resources for the needed information. For example, broader subjects may be used to browse sources, whereas specific terms may be used to keyword search electronic sources. Table 2-3 depicts subjects and terms that are suitable for browsing and keyword searching.

Table 2-3. Subject and Terms for Browsing and Keyword Searching

Broad Terms for Browsing	Narrow Terms for Keyword Searching
Employment Competition Employment Agreement Noncompete Agreement	Time limitation Geographic limitation Same or similar industry Enforceable

Here are some tips for generating subjects and terms:

- Consider the legal significance of the subjects and terms. For example, in an employment law issue, the parties involved should not be described as "Bank Teller" and "Bank," but rather as "Employee" and "Employer," as that is the legally relevant relationship.
- Consider whether certain terms would typically be discussed together.
- Consider the level of specificity that is most likely to be used in primary law. For example, in an issue regarding the liability of a landlord for a cockroach infestation, the researcher should group their research on cockroaches with that of other insects or animals that infest apartments and are classified as pests or vermin.
- Be creative in generating possible search terms.

2. Research Strategy

Once the preliminary analysis of the research problem is complete, the researcher must plan a research strategy for locating the needed information. The researcher must determine possible sources of information, then select the most appropriate sources. The determination of the most appropriate sources depends on which resources are accessible, what information is already known, which sources of law govern the legal issues, and which subjects or terms are associated with the legal question. For each legal issue identified, the researcher should assess the available resources, list the potential authority that may govern it, and consider the order in which the sources should be consulted.

In most cases, it is most efficient to begin with secondary sources of law before researching primary sources of law. Choosing appropriate secondary sources is discussed in chapter 3, but, in general, the researcher's existing level of knowledge on a specific area of the law informs their choice of secondary sources. If approaching a new or unfamiliar topic, a basic secondary source, such as an encyclopedia, will provide the preliminary information needed for successful research. But if the researcher is approaching a familiar topic, an in-depth secondary source, such as a treatise, may be a better starting point.

The purpose of the initial stage of research is to build knowledge and understanding of an area of law. When approaching a problem in a new or unfamiliar area of the law, the researcher should locate both the specific information that may pertain to their research problem and should also review general information and issues relevant to that area. For example, a researcher would be remiss to analyze the rules governing limited liability companies without recognizing that a given business entity does not constitute a limited liability company, meaning that the rules governing limited liability companies do not apply to the business entity. Chapter 3 provides recommendations on how to approach secondary sources to ensure that all relevant information has been located.

B. Executing a Research Plan

Executing a research plan involves locating the selected sources, then finding relevant information within the selected sources using subjects and terms. It is common for the information located during research to require that the research plan be revised or refined.[1]

1. Locating Sources

Although much legal research is done using electronic resources, print resources are sometimes the superior or only available options. The selection of resources is often a matter of availability, although it is sometimes a matter of preferred format or database. Print resources may be less expensive, more accessible, or easier to use than electronic resources. For example, print resources may be preferred when researching court rules, as the process requires simultaneously referencing many rules and reading rules in conjunction.

---

1. For further information about search techniques, see part I.B.2 below.

Choosing an electronic resource requires the additional assessment of access, database contents, and cost. Lexis and Westlaw are the two major legal databases. Other general legal databases include Bloomberg Law, Fastcase, and Casetext. In addition to general databases, there are many specialized databases that contain historical materials, resources on specific topics, news, analytics, and other information.

With so many legal database options, it may be difficult to know which database will contain the needed information. Legal research manuals such as this one, online research guides created by law libraries, law library catalogs, and directories contained within databases themselves may assist in identifying and locating particular resources.

2. Locating Information within Sources

Search Techniques

There are several approaches to locating information within a source. The appropriate choice of approach should consider the stage of research, the type of source, and the extent of the researcher's knowledge of the source and its contents. Browsing techniques are the only available techniques when using print resources. Browsing techniques are available when using electronic resources, as well. Electronic resources may also be searched through keyword searching techniques. A researcher should be prepared to be flexible with their approaches to conduct the most successful research. If a researcher is unwilling to be flexible, the research may be of a poor quality, and the researcher may waste their time.

Browsing

Most primary and secondary sources allow for some browsing, that is reviewing an organized list that directs a researcher to information within a source. Most legal resources provide tables of contents and indexes, which can be browsed to locate relevant information.

The table of contents is a list that reflects how information is organized within a resource. Legal resources are usually organized by topic; secondary sources, specifically, are usually organized to represent the structure of the law. Browsing the table of contents is an effective strategy, especially if a researcher intends to have a broad perspective on a research problem. As the table of contents is generally organized by chapter, part, or section, a researcher can situate their specific research question within a larger context and discover related information and issues.

Browsing an index is an effective, efficient strategy for locating very specific information. Indexes, which are found in both print and many electronic resources, are alphabetical lists of the contents contained in resources. Indexes are useful in that they do not require that a researcher know the general subject under which their specific information exists, and they usually provide alternative terms. For example, statutes of limitation are called "limitations on actions" in some jurisdictions. If a researcher keyword searches "statutes of limitations," it may not produce any results. Locating "statute of limitation" in the index, however, would indicate that "limitation on actions" is the proper term.

Keyword Searching

Most researchers are familiar with keyword searching due to the pervasiveness and extensive use of the internet. Searching the internet is somewhat similar to keyword searching for legal resources, but more advanced skills are required to effectively search legal databases. Many legal databases have interfaces that encourage immediate keyword searching without narrowing jurisdiction, subject matter, or source. However, keyword searching is far more effective when it is limited to a smaller content area.

Legal databases allow for two types of searching: natural language searching and Boolean searching, also known as "terms and connectors" searching. A natural language search is simply made up of a keyword or a series of keywords. A terms and connectors search contains both keywords and special commands or connectors that direct the database to generate results that fit the specific parameters of the search string. Table 2-4 compares a natural language search with a terms and connectors search.

Table 2-4. Natural Language Search vs. Terms and Connectors Search

Natural Language	noncompete agreement geographic restriction
Terms & Connectors	"noncompete agreement" and (geograph! / 3restrict!)

Natural language searching may be useful where a thorough and comprehensive search is not required. Natural language searching relies on a database's algorithm to determine relevant results based on the terms entered. A natural language search will usually return some relevant results, but it is likely to return a number of irrelevant results as well. A natural language search may also generate an excessive number of results that would be impossible for a researcher to review, especially under time constraints.

Terms and connectors searching is typically the more effective, efficient, and thorough method, as it provides the researcher with more control over the results that the database returns. The results of terms and connectors searching reflect the search exactly as entered. Effective terms and connectors searching thus produces a limited number of results that have a high percentage of relevancy.

Most databases have terms and connectors search functionality and have the most basic connectors: AND, OR, and NOT. Many databases, including Lexis and Westlaw, have additional connectors that support extremely precise searching. Table 2-5 lists the most common connectors used on Lexis and Westlaw.

Table 2-5. Common Connectors

" "	Exact phrase
&	And
OR	Or
Space (Westlaw)	Or
!	Root Expander
+n	First term to be before the second term within a specified number of words
/n	Within a specified number of words
+s	First term to be before the second term within the same sentence
/s	Within the same sentence
+p	First term to be before the second term within the same paragraph
/p	Within the same paragraph
% (Westlaw)	But not
AND NOT (Lexis)	But not

The process of keyword searching in a database generally starts with limiting the information searched to the most narrow content area that will return relevant results. For example, when researching case law alone, the researcher should navigate to the case law content area, narrow the jurisdiction, then begin searching. Likewise, when searching treatises, the researcher should navigate to the treatise content area, then narrow the subject area or search a specific title. Limiting a search in such a manner will produce fewer results that are more relevant.

The process of keyword searching also involves developing a search string. The researcher should begin developing a search string using the list of keywords derived from the preliminary analysis of the research problem. The researcher should consider how the keywords are likely to appear in any document related to the research problem and question. Will certain keywords appear more than one time in a relevant document? Will certain keywords appear with varying endings? Will certain keywords be adjacent to each other? Do the keywords have any synonyms that should be accounted for, so as to not exclude relevant results? Do some words appear with varying endings? Terms and connectors searching can account for these variables.

Assessing Results

The final step of keyword searching is evaluating the results to determine if the keyword search was effective. To evaluate the results, the researcher should review the top results to assess whether they are relevant to the question. Next, the researcher should consider the number of results. If there are hundreds or thousands of results, the search was likely too broad. The search can be narrowed and refined by inserting additional keywords, replacing an "AND" connector with a proximity connector, or removing synonyms. If there are too few results or zero results, the search was likely too narrow. The search may be broadened by removing keywords, removing proximity connectors, or adding synonyms.

3. *Effectively Reviewing Sources*

After conducting a successful search, the researcher must read, view, and analyze the information and extract that which is relevant to the question. Careful reading of the information is crucial to the research process, as is careful analysis. The researcher should assess whether the information is relevant to the question and whether it is authoritative, that is, whether it is law that governs the facts of the research problem. Thus, the researcher should consider whether the sources are primary or secondary; whether the law is mandatory or persuasive; and whether the sources provide all the information needed to respond to the question.

The researcher should repeat the process for effectively reviewing sources until all relevant information is located. The goal of the research process, and thus of the process for effectively reviewing sources, is to find and analyze primary sources of law that offer mandatory precedent. Such sources will provide the clearest information to respond to the question.

Reviewing Secondary Sources

Secondary sources are used to learn about the law, so the process of reviewing secondary sources is critical. First, a researcher should take note of certain information in a secondary source including legal rules, exceptions, tests, and defenses. Using a secondary source to gain an understanding of the framework of the law will provide a stronger base of knowledge when researching primary law. It is far more difficult to synthesize an area of law from a primary source than from a secondary source. In fact, the author of the secondary source has already done much of the work of synthesizing. As a result, when it comes time to transition from researching secondary sources to researching primary sources, it will be much easier for the researcher to identify relevant information.

Second, a researcher should take note of the language in the secondary source used to describe the law and related legal issues. The language in the secondary source will likely be similar to the language in the primary source. Consequently, a secondary source is an excellent source for learning effective keywords and phrases for later searching. These keywords should be added to the research plan as they are discovered to refine the search strategy.

Finally, a researcher should be aware that secondary sources function as starting points for finding primary sources and other related secondary sources. A relevant secondary source should yield citations that will progress the research process. For example, a relevant secondary source may refer to primary law in footnotes, bibliographies, tables of cases, and other references.

Reviewing Primary Sources

A systematic approach to researching primary sources of law ensures thoroughness and lowers the chance of overlooking controlling authority. The basis of effective, efficient research of primary law is an understanding of the law that governs the issue and citations to major controlling statutes, regulations, or cases. Without this basis, research of primary law may be inaccurate, time-consuming, and frustrating.

First, a researcher should review the citations to primary sources gathered from secondary sources. The researcher should note additional citations, terminology, and new information to be checked. Although it is easy to move back and forth between sources using links, it is generally more efficient to review each source before moving on. This ensures a full understanding of each source and how it affects the analysis of the legal problem.

Second, the researcher should use the tools in legal databases to discover additional primary law that is relevant to the question. Legal databases, such as Lexis and Westlaw, provide tools like citators, headnotes, and statutory annotations to enable the further discovery of additional primary law. For each relevant statute, regulation, or case, the researcher should employ the appropriate tools and review any new authority located.

Finally, the researcher should use effective keyword searching to further expand the research. Keyword searching is a particularly effective tool for case law, as it results in cases that are factually or procedurally similar.

4. Finishing

In the pursuit of thorough treatment, it can be difficult to determine when the research process is finished. There are several ways to determine that all relevant, controlling law has been located. First, developing a research plan, following the systematic approach of the research plan, and following up on new information discovered during the research process is likely to result in locating all relevant information.

Second, using multiple approaches and techniques during the research process increases the likelihood of finding all relevant information. For example, approaching case law research by following citations from secondary sources, consulting statutory annotations, and keyword searching reduces the chance that any major authority will be overlooked. Finally, at some point in the research process, the same statutes, regulations, and cases will appear, regardless of the search approaches and techniques used. When new search approaches and techniques do not return new authority, the research process is complete.

C. Synthesizing Research

The final step in the research process is synthesizing the research by organizing and presenting the information as a research product. The format, contents, and level of detail of the research product depend on the purpose of the research. If the research product is a brief to a court, the act of synthesizing the research will be much more extensive than if the research product is a summary or email memorandum on a straightforward research problem. When synthesizing, a researcher should remember the hierarchy of authorities, considering the binding force of the law found and the relative weight of the persuasive authority.

D. Updating Research

Before presenting a final research product to a court, supervisor, or client, the author must ensure that all primary sources of law are current and have been verified. Because the law constantly evolves, updating the research results prior to submitting the research product will assure the author that there have been no revisions to the law that will affect the relevant legal analysis. Chapter 9 discusses methods of updating research.

II. Documenting the Process

Documenting research is a critical, but often overlooked, part of the research process. The preliminary analysis of the research problem should be documented in a research plan, and the research itself should be tracked in a research log. Developing a research plan and adopting a research strategy promote efficiency and thoroughness. Likewise, recording the research process provides a method for returning to earlier sources, continuing the research at a later time, and enabling easy updating.

A. Elements of a Research Plan

Developing a research plan promotes efficient research through its systematic approach. A systematic approach helps avoid missing important information or beginning the research in too broad or too narrow of a manner. A research plan also promotes thoroughness, as it provides a clear method to approach the problem, involving initially evaluating the problem and considering it from multiple perspectives, which reduces the likelihood of missing important information. Finally, relying on a research plan is a practical way to save time in the research process. It is not unusual to be interrupted during the research process; having a research plan allows a researcher to return to their work without retracing complex steps.

It is common to learn new information during the research process, therefore requiring that the research plan be revised. The research plan may be revised by updating search terms, limiting jurisdiction, narrowing types of sources, or adopting an entirely new, alternative approach. Thus, a researcher should develop a research plan at the outset of the research process, but be flexible in refining it.

A research plan has two parts—preresearch planning and research strategy. Preresearch planning involves summarizing the factual analysis, identifying the relevant areas of law and jurisdiction, articulating the relevant legal issues, and listing the relevant subjects and terms for the purpose of searching. Research strategy involves listing potential sources and the order in which the sources will be consulted.

B. Components of a Research Log

An accurate research log lists the date, the sources consulted, the manner in which the information in each source was accessed, what information was found in each source, and a follow-up course of action. Maintaining an up-to-date research log is a preferred practice from an efficiency standpoint because it allows for revisiting research without retracing steps. It allows the researcher to revisit sources and information that may not have been immediately recognized as relevant. The following information should be captured in a research log:

- *Date:* Include the date on which the research was conducted.
- *Sources Consulted:* Record the titles of the sources or citations to primary sources of law with enough information so that the sources may be easily located again. If using an electronic database, record the link of the source as well. Notably, Lexis and Westlaw provide options for copying a citation with its proper link.
- *Manner of Access:* Record the search method or keyword search used to locate a specific source. If using a keyword search, record the search string and content area, so that the keyword search may be

replicated. If using an index, note the index term. If following a citation, note the source in which the citation is located.

- *Information Found:* Briefly summarize the information found in the source, even if it seems irrelevant. The summary will help locate specific information again, or it will help prevent inadvertently revisiting a source and expending effort to review a source that was already determined irrelevant.
- *Next Steps:* List citations and other information that may be relevant for later follow-up. It is a preferred practice to note this information in the research log, instead of immediately consulting it. Listing follow-up sources, rather than immediately transitioning between sources, encourages the systematic review of sources that is critical to the research process.

III. Cost of Research

Legal research can be an expensive endeavor, especially considering the cost of legal resources and the cost of an attorney's fees. Careful research planning and a systematic approach to research increases efficiency and lowers potential costs.

Further, although Lexis and Westlaw are the two most well-known legal databases, they are also among the most expensive. Both have features that justify their costs, but there are situations in which a less expensive or free database may provide the same information and search features. The following are the most common legal databases, their best uses, and their cost.

Westlaw

Comprehensive database covering all U.S. jurisdictions and some foreign jurisdictions. Includes extensive library of secondary sources and practice materials, KeyCite, and legal analytics.

Lexis

Comprehensive database covering all U.S. jurisdictions and some foreign jurisdictions. Includes extensive library of secondary sources and practice materials, Shepard's, legal news, and legal analytics.

Bloomberg Law

Comprehensive database covering all U.S. jurisdictions. Includes legal analytics, business information, legal news, docket service, and practice centers.

Fastcase

Comprehensive primary law database covering all U.S. jurisdictions. Includes some secondary sources and an automated citator.

Casemaker

Comprehensive primary law database covering all U.S. jurisdictions. Includes some secondary sources and an automated citator.

Casetext

Comprehensive primary law database covering all U.S. jurisdictions. Includes a brief analyzing tool.

Google Scholar

Case law for all U.S. jurisdictions beginning in 1950 for state cases and 1923 for federal cases.

GovInfo.gov

Contains the *United States Code*, *Statutes at Large*, *Code of Federal Regulations*, *Federal Register*, and legislative documents.

Table 2-6. Cost of Research and Legal Resources

Cost of Research		
Legal Resource	**Researcher Needs**	**Costs**
Westlaw	• Sophisticated search abilities • Citator • Comprehensive selection of secondary sources	High
Lexis	• Sophisticated search abilities • Citator • Comprehensive selection of secondary sources	High
Bloomberg Law	• Sophisticated search abilities • Comprehensive selection of secondary sources • Access to federal dockets	High
Fastcase	• Keyword search abilities • Access to primary law • Some secondary sources	Low
Casemaker	• Keyword search abilities • Access to primary law	Low
Casetext	• Keyword search abilities • Access to primary law	Low
Google Scholar	• Basic keyword search abilities • Access to primary law	Free
Govinfo.gov	• Access to statutes or regulations by citation	Free

Chapter 3

Secondary Sources

I. Introduction

Secondary sources are resources that provide information about the law. Secondary sources take many forms and have many purposes including explaining, updating, and commenting on the law. Secondary sources are critical to the research process, although they are not primary sources of the law, and they can never bind a court.

A legal researcher should not overlook or otherwise disregard secondary sources. Secondary sources may increase efficiency in the research process, improve the understanding of a legal subject and related legal issues; and provide practical information, such as procedural steps, which may be difficult to extract from primary sources of the law.

II. Types of Secondary Sources

Secondary sources are generally designed to accomplish specific legal research tasks. For example, legal encyclopedias are designed to provide brief information about a legal topic with references to more detailed secondary sources and primary sources of law. Because their purpose is to introduce a subject, legal encyclopedias rarely provide comprehensive information about a legal topic. In contrast, a treatise is designed to provide a thorough, systematic treatment of an area of law. Starting with a treatise on an unfamiliar topic is difficult, as a researcher may lack the background knowledge and understanding of terminology required to effectively extract information from the resource. A researcher's choice of secondary source thus depends on the progression of their research process and the information sought.

A. Encyclopedias

Encyclopedias are large works that are intended to address all U.S. law. Because encyclopedias have such a broad scope, they are not detailed, thorough sources. Rather, they are most useful as starting points and as resources that place specific legal issues within the larger context of the law. A researcher should use an encyclopedia when beginning a research assignment with minimal background information. An encyclopedia will provide a basic overview of the law, citations to leading cases, and cross references to other secondary sources.

American Jurisprudence 2d (Am. Jur. 2d) and *Corpus Juris Secundum* (C.J.S.) are the two major national encyclopedias, as they are comprehensive and multijurisdictional. Both encyclopedias generalize the law that differs across jurisdictions and sometimes indicate exactly which jurisdictions differ. Am. Jur. 2d is available on Lexis, on Westlaw, and in print; C.J.S. is available on Westlaw and in print.

Unlike many other states, Connecticut does not have a general legal encyclopedia. *The Encyclopedia of Connecticut Causes of Action* is a reference work that covers theories of recovery under Connecticut law. The work is organized into sections on common law actions, statutory actions, miscellaneous statutory proceedings, and administrative appeals. Each entry includes the elements of the cause of action, information about the statute of limitations, and references to relevant statutes and leading Connecticut cases.

Tip: Review the table of contents of the section in which the relevant information is located. The table of contents will reflect the law in that it will set out a general rule, exceptions, claims, and defenses. It may also indicate related issues for further research.

B. Treatises

Treatises provide systematic treatment of an area of the law. Treatises vary in depth, scope, and importance to the area of law that they address. Some treatises are considered to be standard works, and, as such, they are usually known by the last name of the original author, such as *Corbin on Contracts*, *Collier on Bankruptcy*, or *Nimmer on Copyright*. Treatises group related legal issues together and contain finding tools in the form of tables of contents, indexes, and tables of cases and statutes. They are generally organized to represent the structure of the law and are therefore useful for discovering the framework of the law. They also are useful for their explanation of and references to primary law. Treatises are available in both print and electronic formats.

Treatises are an appropriate starting point for research into an area of the law where the researcher has some background knowledge. The researcher should know enough to be able to search or browse the treatise to locate relevant information. If an area of the law is new, the researcher may consult a treatise later in their research process. Like with an encyclopedia, the researcher should review the table of contents and take note of related issues that may be relevant to their research question.

There are several treatises that focus on Connecticut law. The *Connecticut Practice Series* is a set of treatises and practice guides covering various subjects. The *Connecticut Practice Series* includes treatises on workers' compensation, unfair trade practices, land use, family law, employment law, elder law, and construction law. There are other Connecticut treatises on topics such as insurance, school law, probate, and more. Section V provides a selected list of Connecticut treatises.

Tip: Electronic databases allow for keyword searching across multiple treatises on the same topic, allowing a researcher to identify treatises with relevant information without having to choose a specific publication.

C. Looseleafs

Looseleafs contain a combination of both primary and secondary sources of the law. Looseleafs are most common in highly regulated areas of the law such as tax, securities, and environmental law. Looseleafs are designed to be updated very frequently so that lawyers can stay up to date on new legislation, regulations, and decisions. Looseleafs are so named because their traditional format is a binder with removable pages, which allows for frequent updates to be integrated into the work without necessitating a pamphlet or supplement.

Looseleafs are widely available in print and electronic formats. In certain practice areas, looseleafs are standard secondary works. For example, in tax law, the *Standard Federal Tax Reporter* is a standard secondary work, combining the Internal Revenue Code, regulations, administrative decisions, IRS letters and rulings, and other information. Connecticut has several secondary sources that may be considered looseleafs, although they are often published yearly, rather than more frequently in the traditional looseleaf manner.

A researcher should use looseleafs in the same manner as they would use treatises. Specifically, a researcher should utilize the extensive indexes of looseleafs, especially considering the specificity and amount of information that looseleafs contain. Looseleafs can also be used to stay current on the law because of the frequency with which they are updated.

Tip: Print looseleafs indicate the date of the last update at the beginning of the first volume. Electronic databases provide the same information in the publication information section or within each section of the looseleaf.

D. *American Law Reports*

American Law Reports (ALR) is a singular secondary source in that it is not organized as a typical secondary source, that is, it is not organized alphabetically, chronologically, or topically. Instead, ALR is a very large collection of articles, known as *annotations*, on disparate, narrow legal topics. Annotations bring together explanation with annotated citations to cases in all jurisdictions in which there is case law on a specific legal topic. ALR, although very large in size and in scope, does not attempt to be comprehensive. Unlike an encyclopedia, which attempts to cover all U.S. law, ALR is only useful for some legal topics. Nevertheless, a researcher should always consult ALR, as annotations provide detailed information and numerous citations to case law.

Annotations are updated regularly; even annotations that were originally published decades ago will be continually updated, unless an annotation contains a note that it has been superseded. ALR is published in series, and each series has ninety-nine volumes. ALR is currently in its sixth series. There is also one series for federal law and one series for international law.

Locating information within ALR may be challenging because of its size. If consulting the print version of ALR, the *All Series Index* is the primary way to locate an annotation by topic. If consulting an electronic version of ALR, the index or keyword search may be used to locate an annotation. In order to access the electronic version of ALR, open Lexis or Westlaw, and navigate to ALR under the secondary sources category; alternatively, ALR may be accessed by typing "ALR" into the main search bar for a drop-down menu.

Tip: Review the research references in any relevant encyclopedia entry to locate references to related ALR annotations.

E. Restatements

Restatements of Law are treatises on various subjects, written by experts, that synthesize and articulate principles of common law from all states. They are so named because they "restate" the common law in the form of principles or black letter law. Restatements cover all major areas of common law including torts, contracts, and property. Restatements are revised periodically to reflect changes in the law and society. As a result, restatements are referred to by their series, as with the *Restatement of Trusts, Third.*

Restatements are secondary sources, but they are among the most persuasive of the secondary sources. A court may cite a restatement, especially when the specific area of law is unsettled in its state. Some states explicitly adopt the law as it is written in the restatements. For example, Connecticut has adopted section 90 of the *Restatement (Second) of Contracts.*[1]

Restatements have research value beyond the distillation of black letter law. Each section includes annotations to cases, comments, and illustrations. This information may assist with finding cases from different jurisdictions on a single topic; finding cases from a jurisdiction that cite a specific restatement section; explaining black letter law; or understanding how the law may be applied under different circumstances.

When using a restatement, a researcher should begin with its most recent series, as its most recent series supersedes its older series. Current restatements are available on Lexis and Westlaw under the secondary sources content area. They are also available on HeinOnline, which has a full library of restatements covering all series, including drafts and tentative drafts. It is important to note that older series remain valuable as a source for research into the development of the law, and, as restatements are one of the more frequently cited secondary sources, older cases may refer to older versions of the restatement. Some jurisdictions have adopted law from older versions of the restatement, but not from newer versions.[2] Therefore, the older editions remain relevant.

---

1. *D'Ulisse-Cupo v. Bd. of Directors of Notre Dame High Sch.*, 202 Conn. 206, 213 (1987).

2. For example, Connecticut adopted section 402A of the *Restatement (Second) of Torts*, which made the strict liability standard set out in that section binding law in Connecticut. *Garthwait v. Burgio*, 153 Conn. 284, 289 (1965). Connecticut has considered and rejected adopting a new standard as stated in *Restatement (Third) of Torts. Bifolck v. Philip Morris, Inc.*, 324 Conn. 402, 408 (2016).

Tip: Westlaw and Lexis allow for the use of a citator on individual sections of restatements therefore providing a list of all cases that cite to a particular restatement section.

F. Practice Materials

Practice materials are secondary sources that are intended to help lawyers accomplish some task related to legal practice. Practice materials contain some explanation of the law and related procedure, but also include tools such as model forms, checklists, toolkits, and model language for contracts and agreements.

Traditional practice materials are typically published by subject matter or jurisdiction, or sometimes a combination of the two, and they are used like any other secondary source. Some practice materials focus on one task and cover many subjects. For example, *Bender's Forms of Discovery*, which is available as a print looseleaf or as a secondary source on Lexis, provides model discovery for different causes of action. Other practice materials focus on one subject, but cover many tasks. For example, *Connecticut Contract Litigation* provides guidance for lawyers on issues that may arise in the process of counseling clients, from contract formation to litigation.

Large legal databases have separate practice material sections that are different from traditional practice materials. Lexis Practical Guidance, Westlaw Practical Law, and Bloomberg Practice Centers organize practice materials by area of law, creating landing pages or dashboards that integrate different resources for specific types of practitioners. For example, a practice page or dashboard may incorporate links to relevant primary sources of law, practice notes, checklists for cases or transactions, model forms, and news. A practice page or dashboard may also incorporate state-specific information, including information about Connecticut law.

There are various practice materials that are specific to Connecticut law and procedure. The *Connecticut Practice Series* incorporates practice materials in some volumes, notably in the *Family Law and Practice* volumes and the *Forms* volumes that are cross-referenced with the annotated Superior Court Rules. Other volumes also contain practical content and practical perspectives. The *LexisNexis Practice Series*, available in print and on Lexis, contains several practice manuals covering general litigation and specific types of disputes, such as those within the area of family law. The individual resources in this series are intended to provide practical guidance on courts and procedures, often containing sample pleadings and forms.

Tip: Encyclopedias and American Law Reports *often include references to related practice materials.*

G. Rules Manuals

Rules manuals combine primary and secondary authorities in annotating rules of a given court. Organized by rule number, rules manuals provide the text of rules and explanations, analyses, and citations to related statutes and cases. Some rules manuals also include model motions or forms. Rules manuals are useful for discovering how a court has applied a rule and for understanding proper compliance with a rule.

Wright and Miller's Federal Practice and Procedure, which is available in print and on Westlaw, and *Moore's Federal Practice*, which is available in print and on Lexis, are manuals covering the Federal Rules of Civil Procedure and Criminal Procedure. These manuals are highly detailed, covering the development and application of rules in federal courts. Connecticut has analogous publications for the rules of its courts, the two most well-known being the *Connecticut Practice Series* Rules of Appellate Procedure and Superior Court Rules, both available on Westlaw.

H. Periodicals

Legal periodicals include newspapers, journals, and law reviews.

1. Law Reviews and Journals

Law reviews and journals are periodicals published by law schools. They contain articles written by experts of the law—including professors, justices, judges, and practitioners—and shorter articles called Notes or Comments written by law students. Law review articles tend to take distinct theoretical approaches to very specific legal topics. Many law review articles address emerging areas of the law or predict future developments of the law. For this reason, law review articles are not always the ideal secondary source for legal research, especially for practice-related issues.

However, there are some instances in which law reviews are appropriate for secondary source research. First, for emerging areas of the law where there may be a lack of primary law, law review articles may provide context and insight into how the law may develop. Second, law review articles usually contain an introductory section that explains the relevant area of the law, and law review articles are meticulously sourced and cited. Therefore, law review articles may be used to learn more about the law and as a finding tool for primary law.

Although many law reviews are still available in print, locating relevant law review articles is more effective and efficient with electronic resources. Articles published in major law reviews can be easily located through keyword searches on Lexis, Westlaw, or HeinOnline. HeinOnline is a specialized database containing a very large library of U.S. and foreign-based law reviews and journals. HeinOnline also includes older volumes and issues of law reviews and journals, which may not be available on Lexis or Westlaw. Finally, many law journals post their articles, Notes, and Comments online, offering free access.

The law schools in Connecticut—Yale Law School, the University of Connecticut School of Law, and the Quinnipiac University School of Law—publish multiple law reviews and journals. Law reviews, however, are not jurisdiction-specific, so a researcher should not limit their research to law journals published by law schools in a specific state.

2. Bar Journals

Bar journals are practitioner-oriented periodicals that cover developments in the law, issues in the legal profession, and other topics related to legal practice. Each state publishes a bar journal, and some cities publish bar journals as well. There are also national bar journals, such as the *ABA Journal*, and bar journals focused on specific practice areas, such as *Business Lawyer*. Bar journals are available on Lexis, Westlaw, and HeinOnline. Access to bar journals is often included in paid memberships to bar associations or ABA sections.

There are two major bar journals in Connecticut. The *Connecticut Bar Journal* is a quarterly publication that focuses on developments in Connecticut law. *Connecticut Lawyer* is a more frequent publication that covers new legislation and court cases, information related to legal practice, and activities of the Connecticut Bar Association.

3. Legal Newspapers

Most jurisdictions have legal newspapers that report on the legal profession in that state, developments of the law, proposed court rules or rules of professional responsibility, and other information that is of value to lawyers in that jurisdiction. Legal newspapers are generally published online only and provide email alerts to users for ease of updating.

There are several sources of national legal news. *United States Law Week*, available on Bloomberg Law, is a long-standing publication that reports on important cases throughout the United States, as well as Supreme Court cases and circuit splits. *Law360* is a legal news database that is a standalone subscription product by Lexis. *Law360* reports on dozens of areas of legal practice and provides additional analyses written by lawyers. Law.com is another major provider of legal news, especially through its publication of state legal newspapers. The legal news services of Law.com are also available on Lexis.

The *Connecticut Law Tribune*, available on Law.com and Lexis, is Connecticut's weekly legal newspaper. It reports on appointment of judges, law firm business, and other similar issues. It also reports on major cases in Connecticut and provides summaries of cases decided at all levels of the court and administrative agencies.

III. Researching Secondary Sources

In the overall research process, the first step is usually to consult secondary sources. Depending on the research question and the researcher's level of knowledge, several secondary sources may be required, or one may be sufficient. It is advisable to consult secondary sources when conducting research throughout the progression of a case. For example, secondary sources may be required to research a client's legal issues at the beginning of the case, and they may be required later to understand procedure or to revisit a legal issue when new information is discovered.

A. Locating Secondary Sources

The first step when researching secondary sources is choosing the appropriate source. The appropriate source varies depending on the researcher's existing level of knowledge, the research question, and the sources available. Once the appropriate type of secondary source is selected, the next step is retrieving the source. If searching for a specific source, retrieving it will be a matter of locating it in a database or in print. If searching for a general source, retrieving it will depend on learning which secondary sources exist, then selecting a specific one. There are several approaches to locating a specific secondary source.

1. Databases

Lexis and Westlaw are the two largest legal databases. Although other legal databases exist, Lexis and Westlaw have the broadest coverage of secondary sources, especially of state-specific secondary sources. The following discussion of secondary sources therefore focuses on those provided by Lexis and Westlaw.

Lexis and Westlaw organize their secondary sources, as well as their other content, by type. On Lexis and Westlaw, a researcher may access secondary sources by navigating to the main page; selecting "Secondary Sources" from the menu; then choosing a secondary source subcategory such as encyclopedias or treatises. The researcher may further narrow the choice of secondary source by indicating a jurisdiction, a topic, or both. Once narrowed, the researcher may choose a specific source or use the search field to search within the resulting subset of secondary sources. Although this method prevents the researcher from browsing indexes or tables of contents, it allows the researcher to quickly reference a source containing relevant information. The researcher may employ other search techniques once a relevant source has been found.

2. Reference Sources

Research guides and bibliographies are other options for locating secondary sources. Not all secondary sources can be found on Lexis and Westlaw. Research guides and bibliographies compile all sources on a topic, regardless of their format or publisher. Some Connecticut-specific secondary sources are only available in print, so limiting a search to Lexis or Westlaw may result in the omission of a critical, relevant source.

Many law libraries maintain listings of treatises on various areas of the law. A comprehensive example is the Georgetown Law Library Treatise Finder,[3] which lists print and electronic works on more than fifty subject matters. Although the listed works are located within the Georgetown Law Library print and electronic collections, the resource is still valuable for discovering treatises and, in the case of electronic resources, identifying the databases in which the electronic resources may be found. The Connecticut

3. Georgetown Law Library Treatise Finder, https://guides.ll.georgetown.edu/home/treatise-finders.

Judicial Branch Law Libraries maintain a similar guide with a comprehensive list of Connecticut secondary sources.[4] The list, which is updated regularly, is the most efficient resource for determining whether there are any Connecticut-specific secondary sources that are related to a specific legal issue.

There are other published bibliographies that compile information about secondary sources in Connecticut and other jurisdictions. For example, HeinOnline publishes an annotated bibliography of state practice materials in all fifty states.[5] Subject-specific bibliographies also assist in the process of discovering relevant secondary sources. These may be published, such as *Environmental Law: A Research Guide*,[6] or may take the form of research guides created by libraries and typically freely available online.

B. Using Secondary Sources

Secondary sources are designed to meet the needs of legal researchers in diverse contexts. Understanding the different types of secondary sources, the organization of the sources, and the information that can be found in each will enable their most effective use.

1. Organization of Secondary Sources

The organization of secondary sources aligns with the intended uses of the sources. Large comprehensive works, such as encyclopedias, are organized alphabetically by topic in order to facilitate efficient searching and location of information. Detailed sources, such as treatises, are often organized topically to imitate the organization of the law. Other sources on codified law are organized by code section; for example, sources on federal taxation and on court rules are commonly organized in accordance with codification. Other sources intended for current awareness are organized chronologically, so that the newest material is presented first.

---

4. Connecticut Treatise Index, https://www.jud.ct.gov/lawlib/Treatise.pdf.

5. Frank Houdek, *State Practice Materials: Annotated Bibliographies* (Fred B. Rothman & Co. 2002). Updated periodically. Available on HeinOnline.

6. Christopher C. Dykes & Daniel G. Donahue, *Environmental Law: A Legal Research Guide* (William S. Hein & Co., Inc. 2018).

2. *Effective Use of Secondary Sources*

Secondary sources are typically used to learn about the law and to gather references to additional primary and secondary sources for the purpose of further research. A researcher should approach secondary sources systematically and with a specific research task in mind. First, the researcher should locate the relevant information within the secondary source. If consulting a print source, the researcher should browse the table of contents or index to locate the relevant information. If consulting an electronic source, the researcher may employ the additional strategy of keyword searching.

When choosing a search strategy, the researcher should consider the type, size, and scope of the given resource and adjust their search strategy accordingly. For example, with large secondary sources, such as encyclopedias or *American Law Reports*, browsing the index or constructing a narrow keyword search are the most efficient strategies. With multijurisdictional sources, incorporating the relevant jurisdiction in the keyword search may be the most efficient strategy, whereas with state-specific resources, this would not be necessary. Likewise, large works that cover many topics require search strings that include general terms related to the area of law; but narrower treatises on one area of law would not require that.

Finally, the researcher should ensure that they are using the given secondary source to its fullest potential. When reviewing secondary sources, the researcher should consider the following: (1) any issues, claims, tests, defenses, remedies, or other information that may be necessary for analyzing the legal question; (2) the terminology used to discuss the law; and (3) citations to primary sources of the law and other secondary sources. After consulting each source, the researcher should consider the strategy being used and assess whether the research may improve if the strategy was adjusted.

3. *Citation to Secondary Sources*

Because secondary sources do not constitute the law, it is not common to cite secondary sources in legal arguments. Citing secondary sources may be appropriate in some circumstances, but such citations should be limited to circumstances in which the existing primary law does not adequately speak to the legal issue. Some secondary sources are considered to be particularly authoritative, usually because of the reputation of the author. Restatements of law, for example, are persuasive secondary sources because the authors are recognized experts in their fields and restatements summarize and comment on existing law.

C. Words of Warning about Secondary Sources

Because secondary sources do not constitute law, it is important for researchers to remember the following words of warning.

- Never rely on an explanation of the law as provided in a secondary source. Always consult, and therefore always rely, on the law as provided in the primary source.
- The content of a secondary source does not bind the courts of any jurisdiction. The content of a secondary source should be used to find the relevant primary law that binds the courts of the relevant jurisdiction.
- While some secondary sources are written from a neutral, objective perspective, others are written from a subjective perspective to advance a certain thesis or argument. For example, an encyclopedia is written from an objective perspective, while a journal article is typically written from a subjective, biased perspective in order to advance the author's position.
- Secondary sources may provide commentary that is no longer current due to older publication dates or due to changes to the law that the secondary sources aim to address. Ensure that secondary sources offer current commentary on current primary sources of law.

IV. Secondary Sources in Practice

Legal practitioners use various secondary sources to conduct research, advise clients, negotiate agreements, obtain guidance to litigate cases, or complete other tasks related to legal practice. Ultimately, legal practitioners use secondary sources to stay up to date with the law. Developing a working library related to an area of practice ensures that sources will be available for any research task.

A working library of secondary sources could contain the following:

- **A national treatise in an area of practice** provides multijurisdictional, detailed information on an area of practice. Consulting a national, rather than a state-specific, treatise may lead to an issue that has been litigated in another state, but not in Connecticut. Although the other state's law would not be binding in Connecticut, the other state's law and treatment of the issue would provide valuable insight. Only consulting a state-specific treatise may preclude discovering the issue at all.

- **A state-specific treatise** allows a researcher to locate the relevant law of a state. State-specific treatises often also contain procedural information, guidance for client interactions, and sample forms and pleadings.
- **A news service in an area of practice** allows a researcher to stay up-to-date with developments in the law throughout the United States. News services also usually include longer analyses regarding how the law may develop in the future or how new legislation or cases may impact the existing law.
- **A news service for a jurisdiction** accounts for changes to relevant rules, including court rules and rules of professional responsibility, as well as for information on judges, explanations of issues within the judicial system, and major cases in all practice areas.
- **A rules, procedural, or practice manual for a jurisdiction** provides information regarding court procedure, pleadings, appeals, and other issues that arise during litigation.
- **Practice materials for a practice area and jurisdiction** provide guidance on compliance with the laws of the given jurisdiction. Relevant practice materials that are both practice area-specific and jurisdiction-specific may not exist. In that case, national or multijurisdictional practice materials may assist, but they require verification that any forms, checklists, or other tools conform with the laws of the given jurisdiction.

V. Selected Connecticut Secondary Sources

A. Treatises and Practice Guides

Noble F. Allen, *Connecticut Landlord and Tenant Law with Forms* (2nd ed., LexisNexis 2014). Available on Lexis.

Robert F. Carter, Donna Civitello, Jason M. Dodge, James L. Pomeranz & Lucas D. Strunk, *Connecticut Practice Series: Workers' Compensation Law* (Thomson West 2008). Available on Westlaw.

James I. Dougherty & Louise R. Piscatelli, *LexisNexis Practice Guide: Connecticut Probate and Estate Administration* (LexisNexis 2016). Available on Lexis.

Ralph P. Dupont, *Dupont on Connecticut Civil Practice* (LexisNexis 1998). Available on Lexis.

Thomas J. Finn & Paula Cruz Cedillo, *Connecticut Business Litigation* (3rd ed., Connecticut Law Tribune 2020).

Ralph H. Folsom, Laura Weintraub Beck & Douglas H. Olin, *Drafting Wills in Connecticut* (3rd ed., Lawyers Cooperative Publishing 2016). Available on Westlaw.

Stephen B. Harris & Lawrence Peikes, *Connecticut Practice Series: Connecticut Employment Law* (Thomson West 2005). Available on Westlaw.

Robert M. Langer, John T. Morgan & David L. Belt, *Connecticut Practice Series: Unfair Trade Practices, Business Torts, and Antitrust* (Thomson West 2020–21).

Thomas B. Mooney, *A Practical Guide to Connecticut School Law* (9th ed., Connecticut Association of Boards of Education, Inc. 2018).

Eliot D. Prescott, *Connecticut Appellate Practice & Procedure* (6th ed., LexisNexis 2019). Available on Lexis.

Eliot D. Prescott, *Tait's Handbook of Connecticut Evidence* (6th ed., Wolters Kluwer 2019).

Arnold H. Rutkin, Sarah S. Oldham & Kathleen A. Hogan, *Connecticut Practice Series: Family Law and Practice with Forms* (3rd ed., Thomson West 2010).

Carl J. Schuman, *Connecticut Criminal Procedure* (3rd ed., Connecticut Law Tribune 2019).

Stephan E. Seeger, *LexisNexis Practice Guide: Connecticut Criminal Law* (LexisNexis 2016). Available on Lexis.

Michael S. Taylor & Daniel J. Krisch, *Encyclopedia of Connecticut Causes of Action* (Connecticut Law Tribune 2009). Available on Lexis.

Frederic S. Ury & Neal L. Moskow, *Connecticut Torts: The Law and Practice* (2nd ed., LexisNexis 2015). Available on Lexis.

Marilyn J. Ward Ford, *Connecticut Corporation Law & Practice* (2nd ed., Aspen Publishers 2020).

B. Legal News and Bar Journals

Connecticut Bar Journal

Connecticut Law Tribune

Connecticut Lawyer

C. Law Reviews

Connecticut Insurance Law Journal

Connecticut Journal of International Law

Connecticut Law Review

Connecticut Public Interest Law Journal

Quinnipiac Health Law Journal

Quinnipiac Law Review

Quinnipiac Probate Law Journal

Yale Journal of Health, Policy, Law and Ethics

Yale Journal of International Law

Yale Journal of Law and the Humanities

Yale Journal of Law and Feminism

Yale Journal of Law and Technology

Yale Journal on Regulation

Yale Law & Policy Review

Yale Law Journal

Chapter 4

Statutes and Legislation

I. Introduction

Statutes are laws enacted by legislatures that cover a wide range of subject matter. Part of research strategy includes determining whether statutes may govern all or part of the research question. The statutory research process typically requires analysis of the relevant statutes and subsequent research into case law that interprets and applies the relevant statutes.

Statutory research also requires an understanding of the legislative process, how to locate statutes that are no longer in effect, and how to locate legislative history. This chapter and chapter 5 address these topics, as well as how to research state and federal materials such as the Constitution of Connecticut, state laws, state ordinances, and federal legislation.

II. Statutes

Statutory codes are compilations of the statutes in force in a specific jurisdiction. In addition to the federal statutory code, each state has a statutory code. Although statutory codes tend to have many commonalities, each statutory code has its own organizational scheme and publishing pattern.

A. *Connecticut General Statutes*

The *Connecticut General Statutes* (the "*General Statutes*") is the statutory compilation of Connecticut, containing the legislation in effect in the state at the time of publication. The *General Statutes* are divided by topic into fifty-five titles, each of which is further divided into chapters and sections. Citations to the *General Statutes* incorporate the title and section numbers alone, omitting the chapter numbers. For example, a citation to *Connecticut General Statutes* § 12-40 will direct the researcher to section 40 of Title 12.

The *General Statutes* are reissued in full in years ending in odd numbers; reissuance incorporates all enactments and amendments made since the previous reissuance. In years ending in even numbers, a supplement containing only the year's enactments and amendments is issued. The *General Statutes* are available in print and on the Connecticut General Assembly website, Lexis, Westlaw, and other comprehensive legal databases.

B. *Connecticut General Statutes Annotated*

Annotated statutes are commercially published statutes that include additional information and tools to aid statutory research. The *Connecticut General Statutes Annotated* are published in print by West and in electronic format on Westlaw. A different annotated version of the *Connecticut General Statutes* is available in electronic format on Lexis.

Annotated statutes contain references to additional information to aid with research. The most referenced material in annotated statutes is the *Notes of Decision*, which are lists of cases with brief summaries, organized by topic. The Notes of Decision allow a researcher to locate cases that interpret a specific statute or a particular aspect of the statute.

III. Session Laws

Session laws are the record of a legislature's activity during a year or legislative session. In Connecticut, session laws are published annually in *Connecticut Public and Special Acts*. Public and special acts are published in the order in which they were enacted and are identified by year and act number. For example, Public Act 21-1 is the first act passed by the Connecticut General Assembly in 2021.

Public acts are laws that apply to all people and organizations within the jurisdiction and will eventually be codified in the *Connecticut General Statutes*. The General Assembly also enacts legislation designated as special acts. Whereas a public act applies to all people and organizations, a special act does not. The General Assembly enacts a special act to apply to one person, organization, business, municipality, taxing district, or other limited entity. In Connecticut, special acts are often used to create special taxing districts, water districts, and other government subdivisions. Special acts are published with public acts in *Connecticut Public and Special Acts*, but they will not be codified in the *General Statutes*.[1]

Connecticut Public and Special Acts are available in print in law libraries and in electronic format on HeinOnline. Session laws from 1988 onward can be accessed through the Connecticut General Assembly website. Session laws from the late 1980s onward can be accessed on Lexis and Westlaw.

After session laws are published, they are incorporated in the existing statutory code according to topic. A public act may be placed in the statutory code exactly as it was enacted, which often occurs when the public act enacts a new law. However, a public act can be broken up and incorporated in different parts of the statutory code. A public act may amend one or more existing statutes, and the new language from the public act will replace the prior language. Although statutory codes compile the laws in effect at the time of publication and will continually change, session laws provide the laws as enacted during a legislative session and will never change.

The following describes the Connecticut legislation publication process:

Connecticut Legislation Publication Process

1. The enacted bill is assigned a public act number.

2. All public acts enacted during a year are compiled and published in order of enactment date in the *Connecticut Public and Special Acts*.

3. Public acts are incorporated in the *General Statutes*, which are organized by topic. Sections of a single public act may be placed in different parts of the *General Statutes*. The *Public Acts to General Statutes Conversion Table* is a yearly publication that lists where each section of each public act is placed or codified in the *General Statutes*.[2]

---

1. To locate special acts by topic, consult the Special Acts Index, created and available through the Connecticut State Library at https://collections.ctdigitalarchive.org/islandora/object/30002:o13455915.

2. Connecticut General Assembly, Public Act to General Statutes Conversion Table, https://www.cga.ct.gov/lco/statutes-conversion.asp.

IV. Federal Legislation

The publication process for federal statutes is very similar to the publication process for Connecticut statutes. After the U.S. Congress passes a bill and it is signed by the president, it becomes a public law, which is published individually as a *slip law*. All public laws are compiled and published as session laws in order of enactment date in *The United States Statutes at Large*. The session laws are then incorporated into the *United States Code* by topic.

The official *United States Code* is published by the federal government every six years with yearly supplements. It is available in print and on the website of the U.S. Government Publishing Office.[3] The *United States Code Annotated*, a West publication, is available in print and on Westlaw. Another annotated code, the *United States Code Service*, is a LexisNexis publication, and is available on Lexis. Any other general legal database will include the *United States Code*, although it likely will not be annotated. Table 4-1 lists the sources of publication and access for federal and state session laws and codes.

Table 4-1. Sources of Publication and Access for Federal and State Session Laws and Codes

Jurisdiction	Publication	Database
Connecticut	Connecticut Public and Special Acts	HeinOnline Westlaw Lexis Connecticut General Assembly website
United States	United States Statutes at Large	HeinOnline Westlaw Lexis Govinfo.gov
Connecticut	Connecticut General Statutes	Connecticut General Assembly website

3. *United States Code*, https://www.govinfo.gov/app/collection/uscode/.

Connecticut	Connecticut General Statutes Annotated	Westlaw
United States	United States Code	Govinfo.gov
United States	United States Code Annotated	Westlaw
United States	United States Code Service	Lexis

V. Statutory Research Process

An efficient approach to statutory research begins with an assessment of known authorities and information. The best scenario is to start with at least one relevant statute. Secondary sources often lead to information about controlling statutes, providing citations to one or more relevant statutes. However, if beginning statutory research without citations, there are several strategies to locate the necessary relevant statute.

Statutory Research Process Overview

1. Locate a relevant statute through one of the methods below and read the statutory section carefully.

2. Review the surrounding statutory sections to locate additional relevant sections.

3. Use the statutory annotations and citing references to locate cases that interpret and apply the statute.

4. Use the citator to ensure that the statute has not been amended.

A. Retrieving a Statute by Citation

To retrieve a statute by citation in print publications, locate the volume that contains the title in which the section is found. The titles found in each volume are printed on the spine. Next, locate the section within the title. Print statutes are updated by pamphlets, known as *pocket parts*, that are inserted into the back of the volume. After reviewing the text of the statute in the volume, look up the section in the pocket part to determine whether it has been amended. If the section appears in the pocket part, it has been amended since the volume was printed; the section as it appears in the pocket part is the most current version.

To retrieve a statute by citation through a database, enter the citation directly into the main search bar. Alternatively, navigate to the statute's table of contents to locate the correct title and section.

B. Locating a Statute through a Secondary Source

As discussed in chapter 3, secondary sources are typically the most efficient resources for beginning legal research, including statutory research. It is common that a legal issue is governed by multiple statutory sections, which may be grouped together within a code or scattered throughout a code. Beginning the statutory research process with secondary sources that explain the law and cite to relevant statutes provides the researcher with an understanding of the statutes that govern the legal issue. Forgoing this step requires the researcher to locate and synthesize the statutory sections, a process that makes the researcher vulnerable to overlooking relevant statutes.

C. Locating a Statute through the Index

Indexes are alphabetical lists of the subjects covered in the statutory code. Indexes also provide alternate search terms, which is particularly useful in researching statutes where terminology is precise and may vary from jurisdiction to jurisdiction. For example, in the index to the *Connecticut General Statutes Annotated*, the entry "Juveniles" indicates the alternate term "Children and Minors," as "Children and Minors," rather than "Juveniles" is the term used in the statute.

To effectively use a statutory index, consider the research question in terms of what subject matter is being allowed, limited, or regulated by the state. For example, when researching Connecticut's minimum wage law, beginning with the broad subject term "Labor and Employment" provides a subentry for "Minimum Wages." Similarly, searching for "Wage Laws" provides "Minimum Wages" as an alternative term. In addition, there is an entry for "Minimum Wages" that provides access to the statutes affecting minimum wage. Each of these search terms function as entry points to the statutes, although they are varying levels of specificity for terminology. The advantage of using the index is that it does not require knowledge of the exact terminology used in the statute.

In print statutes, the index is located in softcover volumes placed at the end of the set of statutes. Statutory sections are listed with the alphabetical entries. On a database, the index may appear differently. For example, on Westlaw, the index may be accessed by navigating to the appropriate statutory code and locating the link for the index in the "Tools" section next to the table of contents. It must be noted that Lexis does not provide an index for the *Connecticut General Statutes*, but it does provide an index for the *United States Code*. The index may be accessed by entering "United States Code Service Index" into the search box on the main page.

D. Locating a Statute by Popular Name

Laws are often called by popular names—for example, the Workers' Compensation Act or the Freedom of Information Act. The popular name table, located with the print index or within the "Tools" section of the statutes on Westlaw, provides a list of acts by popular name and their location within the statutory code.

E. Locating a Statute Using Case Law

Case law can be used to locate statutes as well. Case law is generally easier to search than statutes and allows for searching for cases with similar facts and legal issues. In addition, because a court will cite the statutory authority on which it bases its decisions, case law will directly point to relevant statutes.

F. Locating a Statute Using Keyword Searching

Keyword searching may be an effective strategy for statutory research but works best under certain circumstances. For example, keyword searching may be preferred if a researcher has some background knowledge of the subject and understands the statutory terminology in the jurisdiction.

The efficacy of keyword searches improves if the researcher limits the search to a title or chapter within a code. This strategy requires a less precise search and, as it is limited to a smaller amount of information, will return fewer results that are more likely to be relevant. For example, if searching for a statute related to unemployment insurance, navigating to Title 31, chapter 567 of the *Connecticut General Statutes*, which governs unemployment insurance, then limiting the search to that chapter will allow for a shorter search string, as the information being searched all relates to unemployment insurance.

G. Reading a Statutory Section

Statutes are organized into titles, chapters, and sections. Titles are general topics; chapters are subtopics; and sections are more specific provisions under chapters. For example, Table 4-2 depicts chapter 735a of Title 42. Title 42 contains provisions under the broad topic of Business, Selling, Trading, and Collection Practices. Chapter 735a includes sections related to the subtopic of Unfair Trade Practices. Statutory sections are typically organized to be read in conjunction with other statutory sections. A statutory section should never be applied on its own without further research to determine if other sections impact the terminology used, provide exceptions or statutes of limitations, or otherwise limit the scope of the initial section. Related sections are usually found near each other within the statutes. Therefore, when reviewing a statute, it is important to examine the surrounding sections to determine whether they are relevant to the research question.

Though all statutes are not drafted in the same manner, a researcher should remember that there are common elements to statutory schemes that should be considered to understand the complete meaning of a statute. First, the researcher should look for a section that defines the terms used in the statute. The same term may have different definitions in different sections. The section that defines the terms will indicate which terms have distinct definitions, explain the definitions themselves, and state which definitions apply to which sections. Second, the researcher should look for a section that states a general rule, which often allows or prohibits some action. Third, the researcher should account for all exceptions to the general rule. For example, the statute may allow an action, but another section may limit that action. Fourth, the researcher should determine if there are any penalties associated with violating the law. Penalties may include a criminal penalty, a fine, revocation of a license, or loss of eligibility for a benefit. Finally, the researcher should determine how the law is enforced. For example, the statute may designate an agency to enforce the law or may provide that an injured person can bring a lawsuit or submit a complaint to an administrative agency.

Again, all statutes are not drafted in the same manner, but a thorough statutory research process involves considering these common elements. Table 4-2 depicts the components of a statutory scheme.

Table 4-2. Components of a Statutory Scheme

Component	Section
Definitions	Sec. 42-110a. Definitions.
General Rule	Sec. 42-110b. Unfair trade practices prohibited. Legislative intent.
Exceptions	Sec. 42-110c. Exceptions.
Enforcement	Sec. 42-110d. Investigation. Hearing. Orders. Exforcement. Disclosure of information.
	Sec. 42-110e. Appeals.
	Sec. 42-110f. Powers of receiver. Restitution. Judicial supervision.
	Sec. 42-110g. Action for damages. Class actions. Costs and fees. Equitable relief. Jury trial.
	Sec. 42-110h. Class actions.
	Sec. 42-110i. Settlement of class actions.
	Sec. 42-110j. Voluntary compliance.
	Sec. 42-110k. Commissioner's enforcement powers. Court orders.
	Sec. 42-110l. Assistance by court prosecutors.
	Sec. 42-110m. Restraining orders or injunctions. Relief.
	Sec. 42-110n. Consent orders.
Penalties	Sec. 42-110o. Civil penalties.
	Sec. 42-110p. Dissoluton, suspension or forfeiture of corporate franchise for violation of injunction.
	Sec. 42-110q. Service contract agreements. Fee disclosure required.

H. Historical Notes

Following the statutory text, a section called *History* or *Credits* provides the historical record of the statute. As laws are enacted as public acts and later incorporated in the code, the History or Credits section provides a list of all public acts that have affected the statute. This section makes it possible to trace the history of a statute to the version in effect at any time after its enactment, which is important when researching earlier versions of the law or determining when the statute or amendment to the statute went into effect.

I. Locating Cases that Interpret the Statute

Statutory research requires not only a search for statutes and an analysis of how the statutes apply to the research question, but also a search for case law interpreting the statutes. Locating a factually similar case provides more information about how a court may apply the statute.

There are two tools provided on Lexis and Westlaw to assist with locating cases that interpret a specific statute. The first is annotations or Notes of Decision, which are found only in annotated statutes. Notes of Decision are selected cases that exemplify how a statute has been interpreted under various sets of facts. Notes of Decision are organized by topic and subtopic to allow for browsing and efficient location of relevant cases. On Lexis and Westlaw, Notes of Decision are accessed through a link following the statutory text.

The second tool that may assist with locating cases that interpret a specific statute is citing references, that is, cases that cite to the statute. Citing references are comprehensive lists of cases that cite to the statute, regardless of court, jurisdiction, or date. There may be hundreds or thousands of citing references to a statute, which complicates locating relevant cases. To manage large citing references list, a researcher should use filters to limit by jurisdiction or court level and use the "search within" function to keyword search the citing references. To locate citing references, select the "Shepardize This Document" button on Lexis or the "Citing References" tab on Westlaw.

VI. Local Laws

Local laws are laws or ordinances that are created by a subdivision of the state. While the state derives its authority from the state constitution, subdivisions, such as municipalities, derive their authority from charters granted by the state. Charters grant certain powers to municipalities and establish their forms of government.

Local laws are critical to legal research in many practice areas. Local laws govern land use and zoning, define the types of businesses that can be established, and regulate noise, nuisances, emergency services, and other similar matters. In Connecticut, municipalities also regulate the wetlands within their borders and often have separate codes related to wetlands.

Local laws are not published in a standard manner. Most municipalities make their codes available online through services such as Municode or eCode360, but some municipalities still exclusively provide their codes in print at their town halls and libraries. Lexis holds a large library of municipal ordinances from throughout the United States, but it is not comprehensive. The Connecticut Judicial Branch Law Libraries produces a guide to the local laws of municipalities, which is available online.[4] This guide is the most comprehensive source for locating the local laws of Connecticut.

VII. Connecticut Constitution

Connecticut's nickname is "The Constitution State," so named after the Fundamental Orders of 1639, which set out Connecticut's form of government and arguably established the first-ever constitution. The current constitution came into force in 1966 and has been amended several times.

The Constitution of Connecticut can be found in the *General Statutes*; on Lexis, Westlaw, and the General Assembly website; and in the *Connecticut Register and Manual*, a yearly publication on Connecticut and its government. Constitutional provisions in the annotated statutes on Lexis and Westlaw contain the same research tools as statutes do, namely annotations and access to citing references.

---

4. Connecticut Ordinances and Charters by Town, https://jud.ct.gov/lawlib/ordinances.htm.

Research into state constitutional history may require consulting materials related to constitutional conventions. In Connecticut, documentation of the constitutional conventions preceding the 1965 Constitution and the 1818 Constitution are held by the Connecticut State Library; the documentation is available through its digital collections.[5] Also, *The Connecticut State Constitution* and *Connecticut's Four Constitutions* provide historical information and analyses of constitutional provisions.[6]

5. Connecticut Constitutional History Research Guide, https://libguides.ctstatelibrary.org/law/connecticut-constitutional-history/home.

6. Wesley W. Horton, *The Connecticut State Constitution* (Oxford University Press 2012); Wesley W. Horton & Henry S. Cohn, *Connecticut's Four Constitutions* (Conn. Bar Ass'n, 1988).

Chapter 5

Legislative History

I. The Use of Legislative History

Legislative history is the record of the progress of a bill throughout the legislative process. Legislative history may be used as an interpretative tool to attempt to determine the intent of legislators when enacting a law. A bill's sponsor, amendments, statements made in favor or in opposition to a bill, and information learned by legislators during legislative hearings may provide insight into the legislature's intent when enacting a law. The use of legislative history is a method to argue for a particular interpretation of a statute or a word or phrase within the statute.

The use of legislative history to aid in interpreting statutes is not universally accepted. There are several philosophies related to statutory interpretation, the role of legislative intent, and the role of legislative history. Some judges outright reject the idea of considering evidence outside of a statute's text when interpreting the statute, while other judges give weight to the underlying intent of legislators even if the text is not ambiguous.

The use of legislative history in statutory interpretation is common in Connecticut courts. Connecticut General Statute § 1-2z directs courts to use the plain meaning rule in their interpretation of statutes. In other words, courts should attribute plain meanings to words and read statutes in the context of other statutes in order to ascertain meaning. Only if the language is ambiguous or "yield[s] absurd or unworkable results" should courts read beyond the text of the statute for additional information.[1] Connecticut courts have interpreted Connecticut General Statute § 1-2z broadly and routinely consider

1. Conn. Gen. Stat. § 1-2z.

extratextual evidence of statutory intent.[2] Specifically, courts consider "interpretive guidance to the legislative history and circumstances surrounding its enactment, to the legislative policy it was designed to implement, and to its relationship to existing legislation and common law principles governing the same general subject matter."[3] Consequently, researching the legislative history of a statute is common when questions of statutory interpretation arise.

The most commonly consulted legislative history materials are the House and Senate Proceedings and the transcripts of the public hearings held by Joint Standing Committees. The House and Senate Proceedings provide the statements of representatives and senators made when debating a bill or incorporating amendments. Public hearing transcripts can provide insight into information that legislators knew when considering the bill. Compiled legislative histories, which are discussed below, are comprised of House Proceedings, Senate Proceedings, and transcripts of public hearings.

Some parts of a legislative history may be more persuasive to a court as evidence of legislative intent than others. For example, statements made by a bill's sponsor on the purpose or intended effect of a bill are considered to be strong evidence of legislative intent.[4] Courts also frequently consider witness testimony during committee hearings, particularly when the witness has specialized knowledge on the subject matter of the legislation.[5]

Courts occasionally consider other legislative materials to ascertain legislative intent. For example, language that remains when a bill is amended; language that is removed when a bill is amended; and language absent from an enacted bill that was incorporated in a similar, but failed, bill have all been considered as evidence of legislative intent.[6] Less commonly courts consider

2. The Connecticut Supreme Court has held that ambiguity in statutory language "exists only if the statutory language at issue is susceptible to more than one plausible interpretation." *State v. Orr*, 291 Conn. 642, 654 (2009).

3. *Doe v. Norwich Roman Cath. Diocesan Corp.*, 279 Conn. 207, 212 (2006).

4. *In re Elianah T.-T.*, 326 Conn. 614, 625, on reconsideration, 327 Conn. 912 (2017); *Doe v. Marselle*, 236 Conn. 845, 852 (1996) ("We pay particular attention to statements of the legislators who sponsored the bill.").

5. *See, e.g.*, *Republican Party of Connecticut v. Merrill*, 307 Conn. 470, 498 (2012); *Lopa v. Brinker Int'l, Inc.*, 296 Conn. 426, 432 (2010); *United Illuminating Co. v. Groppo*, 220 Conn. 749, 758 (1992).

6. *Lostritto v. Cmty. Action Agency of New Haven, Inc.*, 269 Conn. 10, 21–22 (2004); *In re Valerie D.*, 223 Conn. 492, 523 (1992) ("although no inference of legislative intent generally may be drawn from failure of legislative committee to report bill to floor, weight should be given to legislative committee's rejection of proposed bill

the title and the statement of purpose that accompanies a bill when it is introduced.[7]

II. Researching the History of Connecticut Statutes

The first Connecticut statutory code was published in 1650, and it has been revised numerous times since then.[8] The current *General Statutes* is the Revision of 1958. Earlier revisions include the Revision of 1949, the Revision of 1930, the Revision of 1918, and the Revision of 1902. Although there are even earlier revisions, and some statutes enacted in Connecticut before 1900 remain in effect, most historical statutory research does not extend past the Revision of 1902.

Statutory revisions do not enact new law. Rather, they reorganize and renumber existing statutes and incorporate legislation enacted since the last revision. Although today the *General Statutes* are reissued in full every two years, that was not always so. Researching statutes using *General Statutes* in conjunction with supplements covering many years becomes unwieldy, which leads to a new revision.

Prior to the Revision of 1958, the *General Statutes* were numbered sequentially and were not organized by title, meaning that it was common for statutes to have section numbers in the thousands. Section numbers did not correspond between revisions, so conversion tables were provided in each revision to aid in locating specific sections from the prior revision.

To trace a current statute to its origins, a researcher should begin with the most up-to-date version of the statute. The researcher should reference the historical note or credit appearing after the statutory text, as it provides a list

---

when [1] committee adopted second proposed bill that took directly contrary approach to first bill, [2] both bills were considered together, [3] legislative history of committee hearings contained testimony regarding relative merits and demerits of two disparate approaches represented in bills, and [4] legislature passed bill endorsed by committee"); *State v. Salamon*, 287 Conn. 509, 526 (2008).

7. *Comm'n on Hum. Rts. & Opportunities v. Bd. of Educ. of Town of Cheshire*, 270 Conn. 665, 693 (2004); *Packer v. Bd. of Educ. of Town of Thomaston*, 246 Conn. 89, 116 (1998).

8. Silas Andrus, *The Code of 1650, Being a Compilation of the Earliest Laws and Orders of the General Court of Connecticut: Also, the Constitution, or Civil Compact, Entered into and Adopted by the Towns of Windsor, Hartford, and Wethersfield in 1638-9* (S. Andrus and Son 1822).

of public acts that affect the specific statute. The first public act listed enacted the statute; the subsequent public acts listed amended the statute.

If the first public act listed is not a public act citation, but instead says "1949 Rev.," then the statute was enacted prior to 1949. As a result, the researcher must consult earlier revisions to locate the original statute. The process begins by locating the section of the 1949 Revision, as provided in the current version of the statute and reviewing the margin note. The margin note lists a public act number, indicating that the statute was enacted between 1930 and 1949, or the corresponding section in the 1930 Revision. If the note in the margin is a section number from the 1930 Revision, the researcher should consult that revision, and repeat the process until the margin note leads to a public act.[9] The citation to the original public act can be used to locate the statute as initially enacted in the *Connecticut Public and Special Acts* in print or in HeinOnline's State Session Law Library.

The *Connecticut General Statutes Annotated* provides revision information beginning in 1902, greatly speeding up this process. The researcher should locate the Editor's and Revisor's Notes, either after the statutory text in print or under the "History" tab on Westlaw. That section will provide the location of the statute within each revision and the public act citation of the original statute, if enacted after 1902. If it was enacted prior to 1902, the researcher should locate the section in the 1902 Revision and follow the aforementioned process.

Historical revisions of the *Connecticut General Statutes* are available on HeinOnline and in law libraries in print and microform.

III. Connecticut Legislative Process and History

Understanding the legislative process is important for several reasons. First, when following pending legislation, understanding the progress of the bill through the legislature allows a lawyer to advise a client on the likelihood that the legislation will pass. Second, compiling a legislative history of a public act requires an understanding of the components of the legislative history, as well as their weight and persuasiveness to a court. The documents that

9. If there is both a citation to an earlier revision and a public act citation in the margin, the statute was amended since the last revision, but originated prior to the last revision.

constitute legislative history are generated at certain points in the legislative process.

A. About the Legislature

The Connecticut General Assembly consists of two chambers—the House of Representatives and the Senate. There are 151 members of the House of Representatives and 36 members of the Senate. Representatives and senators serve two-year terms.

The Connecticut legislature is in regular session once per year. In years ending in odd numbers, the legislative session begins in January, ends in June, and is considered to be the *long session*.[10] In years ending in even numbers, the legislative session begins in February, ends in May, and is considered to be the *short session*.[11] During the short session, the legislature is limited to considering bills that are related to the budget and financial matters, raised bills, and bills of an emergency nature.[12] The legislature may vote to hold special sessions to consider bills outside the times prescribed for regular sessions.

B. The Legislative Process

The legislative process begins when a representative or a senator introduces a bill in their respective chamber.[13] At this point, the bill is not fully drafted, but it is a short statement of the bill's intent. The clerk of the chamber in which the bill was introduced numbers the bill, and the bill number, title, and sponsors are printed in the House and Senate Journals. Bills originating in the Senate begin with the number 1, and bills originating in the House of Representatives begin with the number 5000.

The bill is then referred to a Joint Standing Committee. There are twenty-six Joint Standing Committees that are responsible for bills within different subject matters. The U.S. Congress and some states have committees in both

10. Conn. Const., art. 3, § 2; Conn. Gen. Stat. § 12-1.

11. *Id.*

12. *Id.*

13. The legislative process is set out in *Rules and Precedents of the General Assembly of Connecticut*. Although the general legislative process does not change, some details, such as bill filing deadlines, can change. This publication provides the current rules followed by the General Assembly and can be accessed at https://www.cga.ct.gov/asp/menu/rules.asp.

the House and the Senate. However, such is not the case in Connecticut; there is only one committee for each subject matter, and it is comprised of representatives and senators.

The committee may take a few actions with respect to the bill. First, it may do nothing, resulting in the failure of the bill. Second, it may fully draft the bill for consideration by the committee. The committee may also combine the bill with other bills in order to create a new committee bill. In addition, a bill may originate with the committee instead of with an individual representative or senator, therefore constituting a *raised bill.*

The committee may also hold a public hearing on the bill. During the public hearing, the committee hears testimony from anyone who seeks to speak in favor of or in opposition to the bill. Constituents may speak or provide written testimony in the form of *submitted testimony.* Committee hearings are transcribed, made available through the General Assembly website, and archived in the Connecticut State Library. A committee may report the bill favorably, report the bill unfavorably, or make no report. Only if the committee reports the bill favorably does it continue in the process. Joint Standing Committee Favorable Reports do not contain justifications or reasoning for the reports.

After the bill is reported out of committee, the Office of Fiscal Analysis issues a report on the bill's fiscal impact, and the Office of Legislative Research drafts a summary of the bill in plain language. The bill is then returned to the chamber in which it originated for a vote. If the bill passes, it is sent to the other chamber for a vote. During these votes, representatives and senators may state the purpose of the bill and debate its passage. These proceedings are recorded and transcribed, made available through the General Assembly website, and archived in the Connecticut State Library.

Finally, if both chambers pass the bill, it is sent to the governor, who may sign the bill, veto the bill, or take no action, resulting in the bill becoming law after a certain number of days have passed. If the governor vetoes the bill, the legislature may override the veto with a two-thirds majority vote.

C. Other Legislative Publications

1. OLR Reports

The Office of Legislative Research (OLR) is a nonpartisan office within the General Assembly that prepares research and informational materials for legislators. OLR reports are detailed research reports on a wide variety of subjects. They are often prepared at the request of legislators, meaning that the topics reflect current issues and questions. The reports explain the law of Connecticut and sometimes compare it with the law of other states. In addition, the reports include references to statutes, regulations, and case law, making them valuable sources for Connecticut legal research. OLR reports are available on the General Assembly website,[14] and they may be easily located through search engines.

2. Legislative Record Index

The *Legislative Record Index*, published by the House and Senate clerks, details all actions taken on bills introduced each year. It includes a numerical list of all bills and resolutions, their sponsors, and their final dispositions. It also includes a subject index of all bills introduced during a legislative session, making it possible to review bills introduced on a topic from year to year.

3. Summary of Public Acts

The *Summary of Public Acts*, prepared by the General Assembly Office of Legislative Research, is a yearly publication that compiles plain-language summaries and effective dates of all public acts passed each year. Each summary is organized by the committee that sponsored the bill and indexed by its specific act number. The *Summary of Public Acts* also includes a Table on Penalties, which provides the penalties authorized for categories of criminal offenses. The *Summary of Public Acts* is available on the General Assembly website.[15]

D. Bill Tracking

Following pending legislation is called *bill tracking*. A lawyer may perform bill tracking to stay current on the law and to advise a client on how the law may develop in the future. As explained above, each bill introduced is assigned a number, which can be used to track the bill's progress through the legislative session. On the General Assembly website, searching the bill number through the Quick Bill Search returns a bill information page

---

14. Office of Legislative Research Reports, https://cga.ct.gov/olr/rptsbytopic.asp?olrYear=2020&olrTopic=ALL.

15. Summary of Public Acts, https://cga.ct.gov/olr/PublicActSummaryBooks.asp.

including all actions that the legislature has taken on the bill. Westlaw provides much of the same information for Connecticut bills. Lexis provides this information, as well, but it also includes an indicator of likelihood of passage and allows for email alerts to track bills.

Multiple bills on the same or closely related subjects may be introduced during one legislative session. The General Assembly website provides a subject index and a keyword search form for bills. Likewise, Lexis and Westlaw allow for keyword searching to locate bills by subject.

E. Connecticut Legislative History

1. Compiled Legislative Histories

Legislative histories are compiled and identified by their public act numbers, rather than their statutory sections. Therefore, the first step in compiling a legislative history of a statute is to identify the correct public act number by consulting the historical note after the statutory text for a list of public acts that have affected the statute. The first public act that is listed is the original act that enacted the statute, and the subsequent public acts that are listed amended the statute. It is possible that the text of the current statute could have originated in any of the public acts listed. Both the *General Statutes* and the *General Statutes Annotated* include notes that briefly describe the effects of each amendment. The notes usually provide enough information to determine the correct public act; if not, the researcher should consult each public act in full.

When compiling a legislative history, first determine if the legislative history has already been compiled by the Connecticut State Library.[16] The Connecticut State Library has compiled and digitized hundreds of legislative histories, which may be searched by public act number.[17] Legislative histories compiled by the Connecticut State Library include House and Senate Proceedings and public hearing transcripts.

16. Locating a Connecticut Legislative History, https://ctstatelibrary.org/leghistory/.

17. Public Act Legislative Histories, https://www.ctatatelibrarydata.org/legislative-history-bills/.

2. *Compiling a Legislative History*

If a legislative history has not been compiled, the Connecticut State Library will compile it for a fee, or it may be compiled using the print volumes at the State Library or using microfilm for select years at other Connecticut law libraries. The full transcripts of all House Proceedings, Senate Proceedings, and Joint Standing Committee Hearings are arranged and published by date. A card index provides the page numbers on which the bill is discussed within each volume. Full legislative histories beginning in 1953 are available, and full transcripts of committee hearings beginning in 1899 are available.

Table 5-1 shows a legislative history card created by the Connecticut State Library, including all the relevant information required to compile a legislative history.

Table 5-1. Legislative History Card of the Connecticut State Library

Note	Card entry	Pages	Note
Bill and Public Act Number	**Act Number:** PA 19-87		
	Bill Number: SB81		
	House: 9535–9539	5	Page numbers in print volumes of House and Senate Proceedings where discussion of the bill can be found
	Senate: 478–486, 545–546	11	
Committee assignment and page numbers for the public hearing where the bill was discussed	**Higher Education:** 21–25, 41–51, 156, 166	18	
	Page Total:	34	

For legislation introduced in 1988 and later, an unofficial version of the legislative history is available on the Connecticut General Assembly website. The legislative history is not compiled by public act number, and it must be searched by bill number through the Advanced Bill and Document Search.[18] The most effective way to use this search to locate parts of the legislative

18. Connecticut General Assembly Advanced Bill and Document Search, https://search.cga.state.ct.us/r/adv/.

history is to enter the bill number[19] in the "Document Text" search field, choose the appropriate year, and limit the search to "Public Hearing Transcripts" and "Transcripts, Session" from the options at the bottom of the page. Transcripts are organized by date, meaning that the results will consist of full transcripts of proceedings or hearings that occurred on a particular date. Transcripts reference bill numbers in order to discuss specific legislation. Selected transcripts are available on Westlaw by navigating to the "History" tab and choosing "Legislative History Materials." Selected legislative history, including some transcripts, are available by year.

Transcripts found on the General Assembly website and Westlaw are unofficial and lack pagination. Thus, these transcripts should not be submitted to a court in support of a brief. Nevertheless, these transcripts are an accessible means to review legislative history. Table 5-2 lists the parts of Connecticut legislative history in print and electronic sources.

Table 5-2. Parts of Connecticut Legislative History in Print and Electronic Sources

Document	Description	Print Sources	Databases
Bill	Legislation prior to enactment	Individually published	Connecticut General Assembly Website (CGA)
Committee Hearing	Transcript of hearing held before Joint Committees	Joint Standing Committee Hearings	CGA Conn. State Library Westlaw
Floor Debates	Transcript of statements made by legislators on the floor of the House or Senate	House Proceedings Senate Proceedings	CGA Conn. State Library Westlaw

19. To locate the bill number, search for the public act in the Quick Bill Search that appears on every page of the website. That search will return a great deal of information about the bill, including all versions of the bill, the fiscal analysis, the bill summary, the dates of introduction, public hearings, amendments, and votes.

3. *Bill Files*

In addition to transcripts, all bills introduced generate bill files. The contents of bill files vary, but they generally include all versions of the bills considered, and, if the bill was reported out of committee, the plain-language summaries, fiscal analyses, and committee reports. Bill files for bills introduced after 1988 are available on the General Assembly website by searching the bill number or public act number in the Quick Search. Bills introduced from 1911 to 1988 are available in a bill file archive maintained by the Connecticut State Library.

F. Federal Legislative History

1. *Federal Legislative Process: A Brief Overview*

The federal legislative process is similar to the Connecticut legislative process in many ways. The process begins with a bill being introduced by a member of Congress from the House of Representatives or from the Senate. The bill is then referred to a committee based on the bill's subject matter. Unlike in Connecticut, committees are associated with either the House of Representatives or the Senate, and they are comprised only of members of that chamber. A bill that is eventually enacted will thus undergo the committee process at least two times.

A committee holds hearings on a bill, calling witnesses to provide information about the bill and its potential effects. If the committee decides to favorably report the bill back to the full chamber, then it will draft a report explaining the bill, its purpose, and its impact on existing law. The bill is then sent back to the full chamber for debate and voting. If the bill passes the first chamber, it moves to the other chamber to repeat the process. If the other chamber revises the bill and votes for a different version, a conference committee convenes to reconcile the bills. The committee drafts a conference report explaining the compromise. After both chambers pass the same version of the legislation, it is sent to the president for their signature.

It is important to remember that the federal legislative process has been simplified here, and a federal bill's path to enactment may not be so straightforward. Nevertheless, research of federal legislative history may be accomplished with knowledge of the documentation generated during each step of the process. Table 5-3 lists the parts of a federal legislative history in print and electronic sources.

Table 5-3. Parts of Federal Legislative History in Print and Electronic Sources

Document	Description	Print Sources	Databases
Bill	Legislation prior to enactment	Individually published	Congress.gov Proquest Congressional
Committee Hearing	Transcript of hearings held before House and Senate Committees	Individually published	Congress.gov Govinfo.gov Proquest Congressional
Committee Report	Report written by committee when reporting a bill to the full chamber	United States Code Congressional and Administrative News (U.S.C.C.A.N.)	Congress.gov Govinfo.gov Proquest Congressional HeinOnline
Floor Debates	Transcripts of statements made by members of Congress on the floor of the House or Senate	Congressional Record	HeinOnline Congress.gov
Conference Report	Report created by the Conference Committee that reconciles two versions of a bill	U.S.C.C.A.N.	Govinfo.gov
Presidential Signing Statement	Statement made by the President when signing the legislation into law	Weekly Compilation of Presidential Documents Public Papers of the Presidents of the United States	Govinfo.gov HeinOnline

2. Compiled Federal Legislative Histories

Although the components of federal legislative history are easily available, compiling the various parts may be a complex task. When the legislative history is older, the task becomes more difficult, as it may require consulting multiple print sources or databases. Compiled legislative histories—that is, sources for all documents associated with the enactment of a federal law—are sometimes available in print in the form of a book and available through specialized databases.

Like when compiling a Connecticut legislative history, the first step in compiling a federal legislative history is determining the correct public law number. The history notes after the statutory text cite the enacting public law and any amendments. The United States Code Popular Name Table cites public laws arranged by the name of the act.

Compiled legislative histories are available on HeinOnline and ProQuest Legislative Insight. Individually published compiled legislative histories are available in law libraries. The *United States Code Congressional and Administrative News*, available in print and on Westlaw, is another source for selected parts of legislative histories.

Chapter 6

Regulations and Administrative Agency Decisions

I. Introduction

Administrative law is created by a government's executive branch at both the federal and state levels. In Connecticut, administrative law is created when the General Assembly passes legislation empowering state agencies, which are under the executive branch, to create rules or regulations to enforce the purpose of that legislation. The legislation is known as an "enabling act," as it sets forth objectives, then defers to state agencies that have expertise in the subject matters. The state agencies are tasked with enforcing the purpose of the legislation through rules or regulations. Though regulations are subordinate to statutes, regulations still have the force of law. Table 6-1 depicts the relationship between a statute and regulation.

Table 6-1. Relationship between a Statute and a Regulation

Statute	Regulation
Sec. 21a-65 Sale of hypodermic needles and syringes restricted	21a-66-1 Definitions 21a-66-2 Safety procedures concerning hypodermic needles and syringes 21a-66-3 Purchase, possession, control and use of hypodermic needles and syringes

State agencies regulate a wide variety of activities from employment to water quality to professional licenses.[1] State agencies are also the first tribunal for certain disputes, such as those related to workers' compensation and unemployment compensation. Administrative research, therefore, is common in legal practice. For example, researching regulations and agency decisions is required to advise a client on proper compliance with applicable rules. In addition, monitoring proposed regulations is necessary to keep a client informed of rules that may apply to them in the future.

The treatise *Connecticut Administrative Law and Practice* provides detailed information about the state administrative law, regulation and rulemaking process, and practice before administrative agencies.[2] Topical secondary sources also provide good starting places for state regulatory research.

II. Regulations

Connecticut's regulations are codified in *Regulations of Connecticut State Agencies*. The official regulations are published in electronic format only on the Connecticut eRegulations System: Portal to Connecticut Regulations (the "eRegs System").[3] Connecticut regulations can also be found on most comprehensive legal research databases, including Lexis and Westlaw, and on state agency websites.

A. Rulemaking Process

Connecticut state agencies engage in rulemaking when generally authorized by statute or when specifically directed to by statute. Rulemaking follows a prescribed process pursuant to the Connecticut Administrative Procedure Act.[4] Each step of the rulemaking process results in documentation that may be relevant to regulatory research.

The first step of the regulatory process is the responsible agency's notice of proposed rulemaking. Notice of proposed rulemaking is published on a

1. Full list of Connecticut State Agencies: https://portal.ct.gov/Government/Departments-and-Agencies.
2. Vincent M. Marino & Barbara M. Schellenberg, *Connecticut Administrative Law and Practice* (LexisNexis 2016).
3. Connecticut E-Regulations Portal, https://eregulations.ct.gov/eRegsPortal/.
4. Conn. Gen. Stat. 4-166 et seq.

weekly basis in *The Connecticut Law Journal*[5] and the eRegs System. The eRegs System provides recent regulatory activity and offers email alerts for current awareness. It is especially important for lawyers to be aware of proposed regulations when advising clients who may be affected by the regulations.

Once the proposed regulation is published, a comment period opens for a minimum of thirty days.[6] During the comment period, any member of the public may submit a comment to the agency proposing the rule, expressing their opinion of the rule. Comments that have been made on regulations promulgated since the implementation of the eRegs System in 2015 are available on the eRegs System; comments that have been made on regulations promulgated before 2015 are more difficult to locate and require inquiries to the responsible agencies.

After the public comment period, the responsible agency publishes a notice on the eRegs System explaining whether it will proceed with the regulation, its justification, and responses to public comments that expressed opposition to the proposed regulation.[7] Regulations are then submitted to the Connecticut attorney general for review of their legal sufficiency. The notice of the attorney general's approval is available on the eRegs System.[8]

The final step of the regulatory process for a proposed regulation is the consideration of the Connecticut General Assembly Legislative Regulation Review Committee.[9] If the committee approves a proposed regulation, the responsible agency submits a final version to the secretary of state, who subsequently publishes it on the eRegs System. The regulation is effective on the date of submission to the secretary of state unless otherwise noted in the regulation.[10]

---

5. The Connecticut Law Journal is published in electronic format only and is available on the Connecticut judicial branch website from 2017 to the present: https://www.jud.ct.gov/lawjournal/. It is also available on Lexis from 1995 to the present. Older issues are in the Connecticut State Library and several other law libraries in Connecticut.
6. Conn. Gen. Stat. § 4-168.
7. Conn. Gen. Stat. § 4-168.
8. Conn. Gen. Stat. § 4-169.
9. Conn. Gen. Stat. § 4-170.
10. Conn. Gen. Stat. § 4-172.

B. Process of Researching Regulations

Researching regulations follows a process similar to that of researching statutes:

1. Determine that there is a relevant regulation through a keyword search of the regulations, secondary source, or another reference. In Connecticut, the regulation code numbers correlate with the statutory code numbers with some exceptions. For example, statutes related to the sale and manufacture of liquor are found in Title 30 of the Connecticut General Statutes. The related regulations on the same subject are found in Title 30 of the Regulations of Connecticut State Agencies. A legal researcher may therefore use a statutory citation to locate a related regulation.

2. Locate the regulation on the eRegs System, Lexis, Westlaw, or other legal research database. Regulations of Connecticut State Agencies are no longer published in print.

3. Review the surrounding regulations to determine if there are additional relevant provisions.

4. Search for administrative decisions or judicial opinions for further information on the interpretation and application of the regulation. Administrative decisions or judicial opinions can be located using Shepard's on Lexis or citing references on Westlaw. Regulation citations may also be added to a keyword search.

C. Historical Regulations

Researching regulations that are no longer in effect can be challenging. Prior to the implementation of the eRegs System, regulations were published in looseleaf format, so that repealed or revised regulations were discarded. Consequently, there are few sources to consult for older regulations.

There are some tools that can help trace older regulations. First, a regulation includes a historical note after the regulation text indicating the effective date and revision dates. The historical note may provide guidance for locating the previous version and a record of the revisions. Using the dates provided in the historical note, the final version of the older regulation may be located in the *Connecticut Law Journal*.

Second, the *Directory of Regulatory Revisions* provides an index of revisions to the Connecticut Regulations from 1986 through 2015. The publication includes the revision history and dates of publication of regulations in the

Connecticut Law Journal, which enables a legal researcher to locate the text of a given regulation. Regulations promulgated prior to 1986 may be found in some law libraries that retained superseded looseleaf pages, such as the Connecticut State Library, and in the *Connecticut Law Journal*. The Connecticut secretary of state and the agencies that issued the regulations also hold historical versions of regulations.

III. Agency Decisions

An agency decision is issued when an agency hears a dispute between two parties. An agency hears a dispute on a matter only if legislation has empowered it to do so. Notably, certain disputes must be heard at the administrative level before moving on to the judicial level. For example, employment discrimination claims typically begin at the administrative level, which in Connecticut is the Commission on Human Rights and Opportunities.

An agency decision is binding only on parties to the specific dispute, and it does not create precedent that the agency is bound to follow. Nevertheless, agency decisions are a valuable source of information on how an agency interprets and enforces its regulations, providing attorneys with guidance on how to advise clients regarding compliance or preparation for an agency hearing.

Agency decisions are not published in a standard format like court opinions. Agency decisions are published in formats determined by their responsible agencies, and they may be published in different formats over time. Some agencies, such as the Workers' Compensation Commission, prepare reporters, while other agencies issue individual decisions. It is common for state agencies to publish selected decisions or summaries of decisions online, but it is not a universal practice. In addition, it is common for some decisions to be indexed by agencies or by libraries. For decisions issued prior to 2000, these indexes may be the only way to locate decisions by subject.

Lexis and Westlaw contain selected Connecticut administrative decisions, and some other legal databases contain selected decisions as well. The Connecticut State Library provides a guide to state agency decisions with detailed information on locating decisions online, in databases, and in libraries.[11] Table 6-2 depicts sources for selected administrative decisions.

11. https://libguides.ctstatelibrary.org/law/state-agency-decisions.

Table 6-2. Sources for Selected Administrative Decisions

Agency	Website	Database
Connecticut State Board of Labor Relations Decisions	http://www.ctdol.state.ct.us/csbir/main-index.html	Lexis
Connecticut State Board of Mediation and Arbitration Decisions	http://www.ctdol.state.ct.us/medarb/grievancearbitra-tionawards.htm	None
Connecticut Commission on Human Rights and Opportunities Human Rights Referee Decisions	http://portal.ct.gov/CHRO/Public-Hearing/Public-Hearing/Human-Rights-Referee Decision	Westlaw
Connecticut Employment Security Appeals Division	http://ctboard.org/ADLIB asp	None
Connecticut Freedom of Information Commission Final Decisions	https://portal.ct.gov/FOI/Decisions/Final-Decisions/Final-Decisions	Casemaker
Connecticut Workers' Compensation Commission Compensation Review Board Opinions	https://wcc.state.ct.us/crb/menus/crb-opin.htm	Westlaw and Lexis

IV. Attorney General Opinions

The Connecticut General Statutes provide that the head of any state agency may seek a legal opinion from the Connecticut attorney general. These opinions are made public by the Office of the Attorney General. Although these opinions are not binding, they may be persuasive interpretations of issues of state law. If a legal researcher is examining how an issue is regulated by a state agency, attorney general opinions may provide guidance on how an agency applies the relevant law.

Attorney general opinions are organized by year and number. For example, Opinion No. 2019-05 is the fifth opinion issued in 2019. Attorney general opinions from the 1990s to the present may be found on the attorney general's website, Lexis, Westlaw, and other legal databases. Attorney general opinions from 1899 to the 1990s may be found on databases that specialize in historical legal materials, specifically HeinOnline and LLMC-Digital. They may also be found in law libraries in print and in microform.

V. Governor Executive Orders

The governor of Connecticut may issue executive orders by explicit statutory authority or by the constitutional authority of the executive branch. Executive orders have the force of law, and they are most often used in times of emergencies and disasters. The impact of executive orders became clear at the beginning of the COVID-19 pandemic when the governor issued executive orders to close businesses and to limit the size of gatherings for the purpose of maintaining public health.[12]

Connecticut executive orders are published online, and they remain available on the website of the Office of the Governor for as long as they are in effect.[13] Executive orders are listed in reverse chronological order and can be keyword searched. Executive orders of former governors that are no longer in effect, beginning with executive orders issued in 1955, are archived at the Connecticut State Library.

VI. Federal Administrative Law

Researching federal administrative law is similar to researching Connecticut administrative law. The process is generally the same, but the sources that must be consulted are different. In addition, unlike Connecticut's statutes and regulations, federal statutes and regulations do not correlate, meaning that there is no relationship between the title and section of the United States Code and the title and section of the related federal regulations.

A. *Federal Register*

The *Federal Register* is a daily publication that records the activities of the federal executive branch. Proposed regulations, requests for public comment, notices, final regulations, and presidential executive orders are all published in the *Federal Register*.

The *Federal Register* is published in annual volumes with continuous pagination. Each daily issue includes the contents organized by agency, as well as

12. *Casey v. Lamont*, No. 20494, 2021 WL 1181937, at *17 (Conn. Mar. 29, 2021) (finding the governor's executive orders related to the closure of restaurants during the pandemic did not violate the separation of powers).

13. Executive Orders, https://portal.ct.gov/Office-of-the-Governor/Governors-Actions/Executive-Orders/Governor-Lamonts-Executive-Orders.

a list of sections of the Code of Federal Regulations (C.F.R.) that are affected by the contents of the day's issue. There is also a yearly index to the *Federal Register.*

The *Federal Register* from 1936 to the present is available on Lexis, Westlaw, and HeinOnline; on federalregiser.gov; and in print.

B. Code of Federal Regulations

The C.F.R. contains final regulations, organized by topic. The C.F.R. includes an index, although secondary sources are often the most efficient for beginning to research regulations. The C.F.R. is organized by titles, parts, and sections. Each part cites to its enabling act and effective date. The C.F.R. is available on Lexis, Westlaw, and GovInfo; on HeinOnline for full historical coverage; and in print.

C. Updating Regulations

The C.F.R. is reissued in quarterly installments each year. Regulations, however, are continuously amended, so it is important to ensure that the most current version is referenced. The Electronic Code of Federal Regulations (the "eCFR"), although not official, is typically updated within two days of the *Federal Register.* Similarly, federal regulations on Lexis and Westlaw are updated continuously, and they are generally updated within several days of the *Federal Register.* The eCFR, Lexis, and Westlaw will all include the date of the last update of the regulations.

Using the eCFR, Lexis, and Westlaw is an efficient way to update research on regulations. However, after using one of these electronic sources, a legal researcher should review the table of affected C.F.R. sections found in the *Federal Register* for each day following the last update noted.

When using print sources, there are several steps to update research on regulations. First, a legal researcher should consult the latest edition of the *List of CFR Sections Affected,* which is a cumulative list that is published on a monthly basis. Next, a legal researcher should consult the most recent issue of the *Federal Register.* Each issue ends with a list of all C.F.R. parts affected to date during that month. Both lists provide a reference to the page number on which a revision to the regulation is published.

If the C.F.R. section does not appear in either the *List of CFR Sections Affected* or the list of parts affected in the *Federal Register,* then the regulation has not been revised since being published in the C.F.R. However, if the section or part appears in either list, a legal researcher should follow the reference to the *Federal Register* to see the updated regulation.

D. Agency Decisions

Similar to Connecticut agencies, federal agencies hear disputes between parties and issue decisions. Also similar to the practice in Connecticut, the publication of federal agency decisions is not uniform. Selected federal agency decisions are published on Lexis, Westlaw, and agency websites, as well as in reporters. HeinOnline also contains a library of federal agency decisions covering extensive periods of time. However, research into historical agency decisions and documents requires more specialized databases, such as ProQuest Regulatory Insight or ProQuest Administrative Documents. Libraries that function as government depositories also hold older agency materials.[14]

Research into agency decisions, whether dated or recent, has the potential to be complex, as does research into the other materials discussed in this chapter.

14. Federal Depository Library Program, https://www.fdlp.gov/index.php.

Chapter 7

Researching Judicial Decisions

I. Introduction

Researching judicial decisions or case law is one of the most common research tasks of law students, lawyers, and other members of the legal profession. Case law demonstrates how courts interpret and apply the law. Consequently, an understanding of the relevant case law is necessary to articulate legal rules and exceptions, apply those rules and exceptions to specific facts, and conduct legal analyses.

An understanding of the relevant case law involves an understanding of court structure, court hierarchy, case reporting, and the binding or persuasive nature of case law. This chapter explains court structure, court hierarchy, and case reporting. Chapter 1 explains how to determine whether a case is binding and, if it is not, the persuasiveness of the decision on a subsequent court.

II. Connecticut Court System

Connecticut's court structure is typical of most states in that it is comprised of a trial court, an intermediate appellate court, and a supreme court or final appellate court. The federal court structure is similar, consisting of trial courts, intermediate appellate courts, and a Supreme Court.

A. Connecticut State Courts

The trial courts of the Connecticut superior court system are divided into four divisions: civil, criminal, family, and juvenile. The civil division is further divided into divisions that hear small claims cases, housing cases, administrative appeals, and civil jury and nonjury matters. The superior court system is divided geographically into judicial districts and geographical areas. Generally, civil matters are heard in judicial district courthouses and criminal matters are heard in the geographic area courthouses.

The probate court is separate from the superior court, hearing matters related to estates, guardianships, conservatorships, adoptions, and testamentary trusts. Probate court matters are appealed to the superior court.

The Connecticut Appellate Court is the intermediate appellate court. Nine justices sit on the appellate court, hearing all appeals from the superior court. Cases are typically heard by a panel of three judges. The appellate court was created in 1983, and prior to that date, appeals were directly sent to the supreme court.

The Connecticut Supreme Court is the highest court in the state. A chief justice and six associate justices sit on the court. A case is heard by the supreme court if it certifies a question from the appellate court, if the court unilaterally moves the appeal from the appellate court, or if a statute mandates that the case be heard by the supreme court. Cases are most often heard by a panel of five justices.

B. Federal Courts

The federal trial courts are known as district courts. There are ninety-four districts in the country. Each state has at least one district, and larger states, such as New York, have multiple districts. Connecticut has one district with federal courthouses in Hartford, New Haven, and Bridgeport. Federal district courts hear civil and criminal cases that fall within federal jurisdiction.

District court decisions are appealed to the U.S. courts of appeal, which consists of thirteen circuits. Connecticut is within the Second Circuit, as are New York and Vermont.

The highest federal court is the Supreme Court of the United States. The Supreme Court hears cases arising under the U.S. Constitution or other federal law. A party petitions the Supreme Court to hear its appeal through a writ of certiorari, but the Court only chooses to hear a few of those cases.

III. Case Reporters

Courts communicate their decisions in cases through written opinions. Opinions present the factual, legal, and procedural issues before the court, then set out the court's resolution of the dispute through its legal analysis. Opinions are compiled and published in case reporters.

Understanding how to use print reporters is required for accurate legal research and citation. Print reporters undergo a multistep publication process that was developed to make cases available quickly when print distribution was the only option. Reporters are still accessed in their print forms to locate and cite cases, though reporters are now most often accessed in their electronic forms through databases. Chapter 10 provides detailed guidance on how to properly cite cases.

A. Official State Reporters

When the Connecticut Supreme Court or Appellate Court issues an opinion, it is released as a *slip opinion*. It is published individually, identified by its docket number. The slip opinion is available on the Connecticut judicial branch website on the day that it is released.

Next, the opinion is published in the *Connecticut Law Journal* as an *advance sheet*. The *Connecticut Law Journal*, which is available through the judicial branch website, contains advance sheets for the supreme court, appellate court, and superior court, if the decisions are published. Advance sheets contain preliminary reporter citations, and they are released within about one week of the decision.

Finally, the opinion is published in an official reporter. Supreme court opinions are published in the *Connecticut Reports*; appellate court opinions are published in the *Connecticut Appellate Reports*; and selected decisions of the superior court are published in the *Connecticut Supplement*. Upon publication, cases are assigned their final reporter citation, and they are organized according to release date. Publication of official reporters may take several years from the release of the given opinion.

B. Federal Reporters

Cases decided by the federal courts of appeals are published in the *Federal Reporter*, and cases decided by the federal district courts are published in the *Federal Supplement*. Though cases from multiple jurisdictions are published in the reporters, the reporters do not incorporate geographical divisions; that is, cases decided in the District of Connecticut or the Second Circuit are published in the same reporters as cases from all other districts and circuits.

There all several reporters in which decisions of the Supreme Court are published. The official reporter is the *United States Reports*. However, the *Supreme Court Reporter* and *United States Supreme Court Reports, Lawyer's Edition* are widely used unofficial reporters. The unofficial reporters integrate additional editorial content, such as summaries and headnotes.

C. Unpublished Decisions

Not all decisions issued by a court are published in a reporter. Some decisions are designated by the court as "unpublished," "unreported," or "non-precedential." The precedential value of cases and the permissibility of citing unpublished cases in briefs, other legal documents, and oral arguments are governed by the rules of each court.

In Connecticut, most decisions of the superior court are unpublished. Nevertheless, it is permissible to cite unpublished cases in accordance with the format set out in *The Manual of Style for the Connecticut Courts*. The *Practice Book* formerly required parties to submit copies of unpublished decisions cited in briefs, but that rule has since been repealed.[1]

D. Unofficial Reporters and Electronic Databases

As decisions go through the official publication process, they are also made available through unofficial sources, both in print and electronic formats. The most common way to conduct case law research is through an electronic database, such as Lexis or Westlaw. Decisions appear on those databases within days of being released, although the official reporter citations may not be posted immediately. Instead, the case will be assigned a database identifier, which may be used in citations.

---

1. *Connecticut Practice Book* § 5-9 (repealed Jan. 1, 2014).

E. Regional Reporters

Regional reporters are reporters that publish cases from several states organized by region. For example, Connecticut cases are reported in the *Atlantic Reporter*. Regional reporters are published by West, and they contain research tools, such as Headnotes and Key Numbers. Although regional reporters are available in print, researchers most often encounter regional reporters as citations on electronic research platforms.

Connecticut has had other unofficial reporters, such as the *Connecticut Law Reporter*, *Connecticut Superior Court Opinions*, and *Connecticut Opinions*. These reporters, which are no longer published, were the only sources of many superior court opinions. A researcher may encounter citations to cases in these reporters in cases themselves or in secondary sources. Law libraries in Connecticut maintain archives of these opinions. Table 7-1 lists all reporters in which Connecticut cases are published.

Table 7-1. Reporters in which Connecticut Cases Are Published

Connecticut Reports	Connecticut Supeme Court	Print (1814) Westlaw (1802–) Lexis (1764–) Bloomberg Law (1802–) Google Scholar (1950–) Casemaker (1814–) Fastcase (1885–)
Connecticut Appellate Reports	Connecticut Appellate Court	Print (1983–) Westlaw (1983–) Lexis (1983–) Bloomberg Law (1983–) Google Scholar (1983–) Casemaker (1983–) Fastcase (1983–)
The Connecticut Supplement	Connecticut Superior and Circuit Courts	Print (1935–) Westlaw (1935–) Lexis (1935–) Bloomberg (1935–) Casemaker (1951–1974) Fastcase (1951–1975)

Atlantic Reporter	Connecticut Supreme, Appellate, and Superior Courts	Print (1886–) Westlaw (1886–)
Connecticut Law Reporter	Connecticut Superior Court	Print (1990–2021) Westlaw (1998–2021) Bloomberg (2003–2021)
Connecticut Superior Court Reports	Connecticut Superior Court	Print (1986–94)
Connecticut Opinions	Connecticut Superior Court	Print (1995–2008)
Connecticut Circuit Court Reports	Connecticut Circuit Court	Print (1965–77)

F. Parallel Citations

Cases are often reported in multiple reporters, meaning that the cases have multiple correct citations. In Connecticut, it is common for a researcher to encounter a citation that includes the official reporter citation and the regional reporter citation. This type of citation is known as a *parallel citation*.

The practice of parallel citation is a holdover from a time when only print reporters were available. Providing multiple citations allowed readers to locate cases in different print sources. Because case law research is now performed mostly through electronic databases, parallel citation is less important. Cases may be retrieved from electronic databases using official or unofficial citations.

G. Tribal Reporters

There are two sovereign tribes within Connecticut—the Mashantucket Pequot Tribe and the Mohegan Tribe. As sovereign tribes, both the Mashantucket Pequot Tribe and the Mohegan Tribe have their own laws and court systems. These laws apply to disputes among members of the tribal nations, as well as to claims by or against nonmembers that arise from occurrences on tribal land. For example, a nonmember who patronizes a business on tribal land and sustains an injury may bring the claim in the tribal court system, rather than in the state court system.

Cases decided by the tribes are published in their own reporters—*Mashantucket Pequot Reporter: Opinions of the Mashantucket Pequot Court of Appeals and Tribal Court*, *Mohegan Tribal Appellate Reports: Decisions of the*

Court of Appeals, and *Official Decisions of the Mohegan Tribal Trial Court*. These reporters are available in print; on the tribal court systems' websites; and on Lexis and Westlaw for selected years.

IV. Searching for Cases

In addition to the print reporters explained in part III, case law is freely available online and available on all general legal databases. Multiple strategies are effective for case law research, but choosing the appropriate strategy requires that the researcher assess their preexisting knowledge and the best strategies available at different stages of the research process.

The typical case law research process is as follows:

1. Choose a starting point, whether it be a statute, case, secondary source, or even a keyword.

2. From that starting point, locate a relevant case. If starting with a statute, review the Notes of Decision or citing references to locate a relevant case. If starting with a secondary source, retrieve the case through the citation provided in the secondary source. If starting with a keyword search, select a relevant case from the list of results.

3. Read the case carefully, considering how the specific facts, reasoning, holding, and outcome affect the overall analysis of the research question. Make a list of statutes, regulations, and cases that have possible relevance to the research question. Note the terminology used by the court to describe the issue.

4. Review the citing references for the case. Filter and search within the citing references to generate additional relevant results.

5. Review the statutes, regulations, and cases located throughout the original case and its citing references. Repeat this process for each relevant case.

6. Review the Notes of Decision and citing references for any relevant statutes.

7. Use the terminology from the statutes, regulations, and cases to develop a search string to search for additional cases.

8. Case law research concludes when all approaches and searches result in primary law from earlier searches. Chapter 2 provides a more detailed explanation of how to know when the research process concludes.

The following sections outline strategies for locating cases. The most effective strategy depends on the information already gathered, the stage of the research process, and the sources available. Some of these strategies may be combined for an even more effective search. For example, as explained below, keyword searching in combination with locating cases through a citator is an effective and efficient was to locate highly relevant cases.

A. Retrieving a Known Case

A known case may be easily retrieved using its reporter citation. Because a reporter citation is a unique identifier, it may be entered into the main search box on Lexis, Westlaw, or other database to retrieve the case. The party name may also be entered into the database to retrieve the case, although many cases involve the same or similar party names. On Lexis and Westlaw, slowly typing the name into the main search box will provide suggestions for cases that match the party name. Additionally, party names may be searched using the advanced search options for cases.

B. Case Law Research with Secondary Sources

As detailed in chapter 3, secondary sources are efficient starting points for legal research. A researcher can obtain three types of information relevant to case law research from secondary sources—case synthesis, case citations, and terminology.

Secondary sources, particularly treatises, synthesize and analyze case law. Reviewing these sources before reading case law provides a base of knowledge that makes reading case law more efficient. As some of the work of synthesizing and analyzing case law has been done by treatise authors, a researcher can focus on determining the application of the law to their research question as articulated in case law. Further, beginning case law research with knowledge of the law enhances the researcher's ability to assess the relevancy of cases.

Secondary sources are also valuable in that they cite law that supports their analyses. The citations can be used to retrieve cases through links or through searching for citations. Additionally, the terminology used in secondary sources to describe the law typically follows the language used by courts. Secondary sources, therefore, provide effective terms for constructing keyword searches.

C. Case Law Research with a Citator

Citators are tools that link documents by citation. Courts cite statutes, regulations, cases, and other material in their opinions to support their reasoning, holdings, and outcomes. Through a citator, those citations can be used to locate additional relevant cases.

Citators have different names in different databases. The two most widely used citators are Shepard's on Lexis and KeyCite on Westlaw. Shepard's and KeyCite perform the same function of linking documents by citation. Chapter 9 provides information on how to use citators to update and validate research. This section focuses on how to use citators to conduct case law research.

1. Using a Citator with a Statute

A relevant statute provides a strong starting point for case law research. There are two methods of searching for cases that use a statute as a basis—Notes of Decision and citing references. Both methods use citations to the statute to locate cases that interpret or apply the statute.

Notes of Decision, which are available in annotated statutes, contain cases that are selected as examples of the various ways in which the statute has been interpreted or applied. Notes of Decision are organized by topic, allowing a researcher to quickly pinpoint cases that examine a particular subtopic.

Citing references list all documents within a database that cite to a specific statute, including all cases that cite to the statute. Although citing references to a statute may be useful, there may be hundreds or thousands of citing references, thus rendering the resulting list of cases overwhelming. However, there are tools that allow a researcher to narrow the list of cases to fewer relevant cases.

First, filters may be used to limit the results by jurisdiction and date. Second, Lexis and Westlaw provide a "search within" feature that allows for keyword searches to be performed within citing references. Keyword searching within citing references, rather than keyword searching all cases, is a strategy to locate highly relevant cases. Because the information being searched has already been narrowed to only cases that cite the relevant statute, keyword searching can be more efficient, and the resulting list of cases will be shorter with a higher percentage of relevant cases.

2. *Using a Citator with a Relevant Case*

Judges often refer to statutes, regulations, and earlier cases to support their decisions. Therefore, a relevant decision will cite primary law that is likely relevant to the given research question. Consequently, locating a highly relevant case will lead to additional relevant primary law cited within the decision. Further, later cases with similar facts and legal issues may cite the case. Locating later cases that cite the original, relevant case is the primary function of the citator.

To use the citator on Lexis, select "Shepardize This Document"; to use the citator on Westlaw, select the "Citing References" tab. The citator will present a list of all cases within the database that cite the original case.

Using a citator to research case law is highly effective, but like with statutes, there may be hundreds or thousands of citing references. When reviewing a case's citing references, there are several tools that may help to quickly focus on relevant cases:

- **Depth of Treatment** indicates the depth of the analysis given to the original case. A visual indicator ranges from one bar to four bars, with four bars representing the most in-depth treatment. Filtering or sorting by depth of treatment narrows the citing cases to only those with substantial discussions of the original case.
- **"Search Within"** allows for a keyword search of the citing references. "Search within" allows the researcher to find highly relevant cases, as the search is conducted within cases that cite the original case. This method is very effective for locating factually similar cases and cases on narrow subtopics.
- **Court Level** organizes citing references from highest to lowest court, which is useful when searching for binding appellate decisions, as the results may be filtered to identify cases from courts of a certain level.
- **Headnotes** summarize the legal issues within cases. Lexis and Westlaw provide a headnotes filter, which narrows the results to only those including specific legal issues. This is useful when the researcher focuses on a narrow legal issue, as the filter removes cases that do not address that legal issue.

Tip: The above tools may be combined for further refinement of results. For example, a keyword search may be executed within a list of citing cases, which may be sorted by depth of treatment. The results would then include only those that cite the original case, contain relevant keywords, and begin with the cases that provide the most analysis of the original case.

D. Digests, Headnotes, and Key Numbers

A digest is a tool for locating case law. At the most basic level, digests are very large subject indexes. Digests organize cases by legal issue in a hierarchical manner. Each case listed in the index is *digested* or very briefly summarized. Headnotes and Key Numbers are additional tools that are embedded in the structure of the digest.

1. Digests

The *Connecticut Digest* is the primary digest for Connecticut cases. Connecticut cases are included in other digests, such as the *Atlantic Digest*, which is the digest for the *Atlantic Reporter*, and the *Decennial Digest*, which is the digest for all states that covers ten-year spans. Digests have not become obsolete with the prevalence of electronic research. The form of the digest has changed for use within databases, rather than within print books, but the purpose of the digest remains the same.

Lexis and Westlaw both include indexes that allow for browsing by topic. Cases are organized under topics and subtopics, and, like with citing references, a list of cases under a subtopic may be filtered and searched for further refinement. On Lexis, select the "Topics" tab on the main page to access the index; on Westlaw, select the "Topics & Key Numbers" link on the main page.

2. Headnotes and Key Numbers

A case published by LexisNexis or West will include additional information before the text of the case that describes the legal issues within the case, in the form of short summaries called *headnotes*. Headnotes are numbered, and corresponding numbers appear in the text of the case to assist with locating the discussion of a specific issue within the case.

On Westlaw, headnotes are accompanied by *Key Numbers*, which are part of the organizational system within the West Digest System. Key Numbers are assigned to topics and subtopics to facilitate the location of specific information. Key Numbers are hierarchical to allow for locating topics with varying levels of specificity. Lexis also provides hierarchical topics in its headnotes.

Headnotes and Key Numbers have two important purposes. First, when evaluating whether a case may be relevant, the headnotes will indicate whether the case addresses a relevant legal issue. Second, headnotes and Key Number are tools for locating cases, thus improving the process of case law research.

Using Headnotes to Locate Cases

1. Locate a relevant case through a secondary source, statutory annotation, or keyword search.

2. Review the case and identify the headnotes that outline the legal issues that are relevant to the research.

3. For cases on similar topics:

- On Lexis, review the hierarchical list above the headnote. Choose the term that is the most similar to the subject of the present research in order to locate other cases within that subject. Narrow by jurisdiction or date, or search within the results for further refinement.
- On Westlaw, review the hierarchical list of Key Numbers to the right of the headnote, and select the topic that is the most similar to the subject of the present research. The results will default to the jurisdiction of the original case, but they can be expanded to other jurisdictions. Additional filters and a "search within" feature may be used as well.

4. For a very closely related case:

- On Lexis, select the link labeled "Shepardize—Narrow by this Headnote." The results will consist of only cases that have cited the original case and include the same headnote. The results will likely be few but will likely be relevant.
- On Westlaw, select the link to other cases that cite the headnote, which will appear below the headnote if any other cases contain the same headnote. Again, the results will likely be few but will likely be relevant.

E. Keyword Searching

Keyword searching is an effective method for searching case law. However, keyword searching should not always be the first strategy employed when researching case law. Other methods—such as beginning with secondary sources or using the research tools that accompany cases, statutes, and regulations—are usually more efficient. Nevertheless, keyword searching is an effective strategy in the following situations.

1. To Locate Factually Similar Cases

Locating cases with similar facts provides insight into how courts have applied the law in specific circumstances. Although secondary sources provide explanations of the law generally, they typically do not apply the law to various sets of facts. Case law, however, describes the facts of each case, allowing a researcher to locate cases with factual similarities and similar legal issues.

Keyword searching is an effective way to locate cases with similar facts, as terminology from the facts can be included in the keyword search. When keyword searching, consider how courts are likely to describe the facts. In other words, the researcher should categorize specific facts as legally relevant terms. Chapter 2 explains how to generate effective search terms.

2. When There Is Not a Known Relevant Statute or Case

Not all legal issues are addressed in secondary sources, especially if the issues are very narrow or unique under state law. In those circumstances, a researcher may begin case law research without any citations. It is possible for the researcher to use keyword searching to locate authority on the issue, but it may be challenging.

Advanced searching, or terms and connectors searching, is the most effective way to search case law. There are several strategies that may be used under the method of advanced searching when the researcher does not have background information or citations. The researcher may search for factually similar cases, as discussed above. A factually similar case may provide information about the legal issues associated with the facts and provide a starting point for researching those issues.

The researcher may also construct a keyword search around the legal issue. In constructing a keyword search for legal issues, the researcher should include word variations to account for possible variations in terminology. Also, proximity connectors, term frequency, and similar search techniques will return fewer, but more relevant, results.

3. To Ensure a Comprehensive Search

A complete research process should include keyword searches of cases to ensure that all relevant cases have been found. Beginning with a secondary source, then using techniques, such as following citing references, statutory annotations, and searching by headnotes and Key Numbers, produces fairly complete research. The final step of keyword searching case law provides confirmation that all relevant cases have been found.

Incorporating keyword searching at the end of the research process is far more efficient than beginning with keyword searching, as the research will have already located the statutes, regulations, leading cases, and relevant terminology. This knowledge will assist in constructing a precise, effective search and in effectively evaluating the search results.

4. Evaluating Search Results

The goal of keyword searching is to retrieve as many relevant cases and exclude as many irrelevant cases as possible. Effective keyword searching takes practice, and it requires continual evaluation of the results to determine whether the search has been effective. Part of the process of keyword searching is reviewing the results to determine whether the search successfully returned relevant cases.

The number of results returned in a search may indicate search effectiveness. If the number of results exceeds several hundred, a narrower search should be employed. Replacing "AND" connectors with proximity connectors, replacing the originally searched keywords with more precise keywords, or limiting the results to only appellate cases are all methods of narrowing a search. If there are very few results, broaden the search by changing phrases in quotations to keywords connected with proximity connectors, expanding the range of proximity connectors, or generating synonyms or alternative keywords.

The relevance of the first several cases in a list of results may also indicate the effectiveness of a search. Search results are ranked by relevancy as a default; if the first several cases are not relevant, the keywords may be incorrect or otherwise improper. To improve the search, return to a secondary source for information about relevant terminology, update the search using alternative keywords, or add new keywords that are relevant to the question. Further, if only the first several cases are relevant, consider which keywords or phrases the cases share and develop a new search using those terms.

F. Updating and Validating Cases

It is imperative to update and validate case law used for legal research. Case law constantly evolves, and the law as stated in a case may be overturned, limited, or otherwise refined. Citators, in addition to being research tools, allow researchers to examine how subsequent cases have treated the original case and therefore ensure that it remains good law. Chapter 9 explains citators and their proper use.

V. Dockets

A docket is the record of documents filed during the pendency of a court case. In a civil case, a docket generally includes the complaint, answer, motions, briefs, and court rulings. Dockets may be valuable in locating examples of court documents filed in similar cases; performing competitive intelligence research on opposing counsel, parties, or potential clients; or researching how judges tend to rule on different types of issues or how long they typically take to rule.

In Connecticut, dockets are available without cost on the judicial branch website under "Case Look-Up."[2] Cases are searchable by docket number, party name, or attorney name. The docket lists the party names, counsel who appeared on behalf of the parties, names of the documents filed, filing dates, and upcoming court dates. The full text of the documents is available for most cases filed since the 2010s. Documents from older dockets are more difficult to locate and, depending on the amount of time that has elapsed, may not be available.

Federal dockets are available through a system called PACER, which is administered by the federal judiciary. Unlike Connecticut state court dockets, there is a charge for retrieving dockets and documents on PACER. Many commercial databases also provide access to dockets. Bloomberg Law, Lexis Court Link, Westlaw Dockets, Fastcase Docket Alarm, and other databases provide access to dockets, although often for a fee.

2. Connecticut Judicial Branch Case Look-Up, https://www.jud.ct.gov/jud2.htm.

VI. Records and Briefs

The documents filed when a case is at the appellate level consist of the record, which are filings from the trial court that are provided to the appellate court on appeal, and the briefs, which are filed by the parties. The records and briefs of a case are sources of information about the case and insight into the court's decision. Further, for older cases, the record is the most accessible route, and sometimes the only route, for locating documents filed in the trial court.

There are records and briefs for Connecticut appellate cases beginning in the late 1800s, although the format has changed over time. The earliest briefs filed in the Connecticut Supreme Court are available at the Connecticut State Library. Records and briefs beginning in 1900 were published in print volumes, until the format changed to exclusively microfiche in 1986. In 2017, the appellate court and the supreme court instituted mandatory e-filing, resulting in electronic availability of records and briefs through the judicial branch website's Case Look-Up.

Briefs available in print and on microfiche are organized by the term in which they are argued. To locate the records and briefs for a case, a researcher should consult the opinion to determine the argue date. Next, the researcher should locate the records and briefs for that month and year, and, within the date range, locate the case alphabetically by party name. Briefs available on the judicial branch website's Case Look-Up may be searched by party name or docket number.

Commercial databases often provide some briefs, especially for cases decided in 2000 and later. On Lexis and Westlaw, a case's underlying filings can be found through links from the case's opinion. U.S. Supreme Court records and briefs are available through specialty databases, such as ProQuest Supreme Court Insight and Making of Modern Law Supreme Court Records and Briefs. Records and briefs from the federal courts of appeals are not as accessible, but those of some circuits are available through the database The Making of Modern Law: Landmark Records from the US Court of Appeals, 1950–1980 and on microfiche in law libraries. *A Union List of Appellate Records and Briefs*[3] provides full information on libraries that hold collections of records and briefs from all jurisdictions.

3. Michael Whiteman & Peter Scott Campbell, *A Union List of Appellate Court Records and Briefs: Federal and State* (2nd ed., William S. Hein & Co., Inc. 2017).

Chapter 8

Reading and Briefing Judicial Opinions

During the research process, a legal researcher will locate cases, otherwise known as judicial opinions or judicial decisions. This chapter provides instruction for effectively and efficiently reading a case and for understanding the essential elements of a case.

I. Reading Cases

Because of the volume and importance of cases in a common law system, it is critical to be able to effectively and efficiently read a case. The following strategies provide a framework for thorough analysis of a case.

A. Context

Before reading the first word of a case, a researcher should consider where they are in their research or in their course of study. Placing a case in context will emphasize the relevance of the case and improve reading efficiency. For example, a student may consider a case in the context of a course of study by referring to the syllabus, to the casebook table of contents, and then to the case itself. This practice may allow the student to improve their understanding of the case in the larger context of the law.

B. Preview

Before reading a case in great depth, a researcher should skim the case in order to understand the court's general focus and trajectory of reasoning in relation to its ultimate holding. The practice of skimming will allow the researcher to pass over unimportant details or to avoid tangents.

C. Structure

In reading a case, a researcher should follow the pattern that courts typically use when writing an opinion. Knowing this pattern will allow the researcher to distinguish between parts of the opinion, and it will improve the researcher's understanding of the decision. An opinion often proceeds in the following sequence: synopsis, statement of facts, statement of precedent, application or distinction of the precedent to the facts, reasoning, holding, outcome, and concurring opinion(s) and/or dissenting opinion(s). The parts of a case are defined below.

D. Key Terms

A researcher's ability to recognize key terms in a case will make their reading more efficient by allowing them to identify and focus on the most important parts of the case. For example, where a court writes, "the facts are as follows," the court summarizes the facts found by a trial court. A researcher should pay close attention to that phrase and others such as "Petitioner/Respondent/Plaintiff/Defendant argues," which indicate the court's articulation of the respective party's claims. Even more importantly, a researcher should pay close attention to the phrase "precedent holds"; it provides the court's analysis of the law in deciding whether to apply that law, following *stare decisis*, or whether to distinguish the case, declining to follow *stare decisis.*

II. Briefing Cases

It is helpful to law students, lawyers, and other legal professionals to brief cases for many reasons. The term "brief" refers to two products—one is a written legal argument that lawyers submit to courts, and the other is a summary of a case that law students or lawyers write to facilitate their recollection of, understanding of, and engagement with a case. Chapter 11 identifies the former type of brief as an example of persuasive writing; this chapter focuses on the latter type of brief, and it explains how to construct a case brief, using the word as both a noun and a verb.

A. Format

A brief should be brief. It should be short enough to be used as a summary or reminder of a case, without requiring the entire case to be re-read. It should also be short enough to be used for discussion without having to refer to multiple pages. Instructors or supervisors may specify a preferred format, including a preferred length, for briefs. Absent those instructions, briefs should be drafted according to format provided in this chapter. Above all, briefs should be useful to the law students, lawyers, and other members of the legal profession in need of the information conveyed in cases. Consequently, researchers should select a format for their briefs that will facilitate their ability to remember, understand, and discuss a given case.

B. Purposes of Case Briefs

Preparing a brief (or "briefing a case") serves a few purposes. First, briefing will improve the researcher's understanding of a case by requiring them to identify the key elements of the case. Selecting the key elements will promote accurate analysis. Second, preparing a brief, and later accessing it, will enable the researcher to discuss the case with an instructor or supervisor with the benefit of having organized notes that conform to their expectations. Third, a brief serves as a reminder of a case that can be consulted to avoid re-reading the case. If the researcher maintains a research log as described in chapter 2, briefs can be integrated into the given document for reference.

C. Elements of a Case Brief

- **Title:** Include the name of the case and its citation. Note the court that issued the opinion, including its jurisdiction and level, and the year in which the case was decided, which may differ from the year in which the case was argued.
- **Parties:** Identify the parties to the case and their relationships to one another.
- **Facts:** Describe the legally important facts and other facts that assist in thoroughly describing the case.
- **Procedural history:** Summarize the procedure of the case, including claims presented to the lower courts, decisions of the lower courts, reasoning of the lower courts, and claimed errors for appeal.

- **Issue(s):** Identify the issue(s) that the court addresses. The issue should be framed as a question that includes the legally important facts and law. It is important to note that, in an appellate case, the court must address whether the lower court made an error in its decision.

- **Holding:** Identify the court's answer to the issue(s) and the court's decision, which ultimately dictates the outcome of the case.

- **Reasoning:** Narrate the court's rationale. Summarize key precedent and explain whether the court analogized or distinguished the current facts and precedent. If there are multiple legal claims or issues, dedicate a separate section within the reasoning to each claim.

- **Rule:** State the principle of law that can be derived or formulated from the case. Advocates may develop broad or narrow rules, depending on the desired applicability of the case to a subsequent case. Because rules are elastic, it is beneficial to develop both a broad rule and a narrow rule for each brief.

- **Concurring and/or dissenting opinions:** Note whether concurring and/or dissenting opinions follow the opinion. A concurring opinion (or "concurrence") is a separate opinion of a judge who voted with the majority but was influenced by a different rationale(s). The concurring opinion explains their different rationale(s). A dissenting opinion (or "dissent") is a separate opinion of a judge who voted against the majority. The dissenting opinion explains their vote, citing reasons for the disagreement. It is beneficial to identify the key principles of concurring and/or dissenting opinions in the brief.

- ***Dicta*:** Note statements that go beyond the facts of the case and/or are unnecessary to the court's decision. These extraneous statements are considered obiter dicta and are not binding precedent for subsequent cases.

- **Summary:** Include a one-line summary of the narrative and the decision of the case.

- **Critical analysis:** Conclude the brief with critical analysis. Is the decision fair? Is it efficient? Answering these and other questions will prepare the reader to discuss the case with others in an insightful manner.

Chapter 9

Updating and Validating Research

I. Introduction

The final phase in the legal research process is to update the research results and validate the law. The law constantly evolves, making it essential to ensure that the research results supporting a legal analysis remain valid. Updating and validating sources of primary law is a matter of professional legal ethics. For example, when a lawyer submits a document to a court that relies on primary law, the lawyer certifies to the court that the law is current and valid.[1] If the lawyer relies on an overturned case or makes an inaccurate statement of law because of a failure to update the research results, the lawyer violates the Rules of Professional Conduct and may even damage a client's case and likelihood of success.

II. Validating Research through Citators

Citators are tools used to update and validate sources of primary law. Citators gather cases that cite a particular case and provide signals that indicate whether subsequent cases affect the precedential value of that case. Citators can also be used to determine whether a subsequent case invalidates or otherwise questions the constitutionality of a particular statute or to determine whether legislation has been enacted or is pending that would amend the statute. Citators thus save a tremendous amount of time that would be spent searching for cases, statutes, or pending legislation.

1. "A lawyer shall not knowingly . . . make a false statement of fact or law to a tribunal. . . ." Conn. R. Prof. Conduct 3.3(a)(1).

The process of using a citator is commonly called *Shepardizing* or *KeyCiting*, which are terms that refer to the two most well-known citators provided by Lexis and Westlaw, respectively. The process of using a citator involves identifying a case or statute to validate; reviewing later cases that cite to the original case or statute; and aided by *signals*, determining the effect of the later cases. Citators are therefore validation tools as well as research tools that can be used to find relevant primary and secondary law.

A. Updating Cases

Citators provide information about cases through *direct history* and through *citing references*. Direct history provides citations to later decisions in the same case involving the same parties. For example, if the Connecticut Appellate Court issued a decision, then the Connecticut Supreme Court reversed that decision, the outcomes would be represented in the direct history.

A later decision in a different case may also impact the original case. For example, a court deciding a different case may cite to the original case and question its validity, narrow its impact, or completely overturn it. The information regarding a later decision in a different case is derived from citing references, which are references to later decisions that cite the original case. Table 9-1 illustrates the difference between direct history and indirect history.

Table 9-1. Direct History vs. Indirect History

Direct History	Indirect History
State v. Joyce, 30 conn. App. 164 (1993).	Purzvcki v. Town of Fairfield, 244 Conn. 101 (1998).
↓	↓
Reversed by State v. Joyce, 229 Conn. 10 (1994).	*Overruled by* Haynes v. City of Middletown, 314 Conn. 303 (2014).

Regardless of the origin of the citator information, the purpose of the citator information is to signal the impact of later cases on an original case. Shepard's and KeyCite provide visual signals to assist researchers in quickly locating later cases that may have a negative impact on the original case. The signals, described below, are displayed prominently near the case name. Shepard's and KeyCite also provide a notation that explains why the signal was assigned and a link to the case or statute that prompted the signal.

Although citators are helpful and efficient tools, they do not replace reading cases and making professional judgments about those cases' impact on the original case. Such professional judgments require a complete understanding of the binding law and a thorough reading of the original case and the later cases in order to ascertain whether the treatment impacts the law that is being relied on.

How to Use a Citator to Validate Cases:

1. When reviewing a case, take note of whether a signal is assigned.

2. If the signal is red or yellow, view the citator report by selecting "Shepardize This Document" in Lexis or "Negative History" in Westlaw.

3. Begin reviewing the citator report with the case marked "Reason for Shepard's Signal" or "Most Negative," then read the case carefully.

4. Determine what impact the case has on the original case and determine whether the case impacts the law as it applies to the research question.

5. Make the same determinations for the remaining cases that indicate negative treatment.

6. Make any necessary adjustments to the research plan to account for the citator information, including notation of any new relevant cases.

B. Citator Signals for Cases

1. Most Negative: Red Flag or Stop Sign

A red flag or red stop sign mean that some part of the case is no longer valid law. A red flag or red stop sign means that the case was directly reversed by a higher court; that at least one point of law was overturned in a later case; or that legislation has been enacted that invalidates the law as stated in the case. The signals do not mean that the entire case is invalid and thus should not be cited, but they are signals that the case should be carefully reviewed and that citations to the case should be made with caution.

2. Negative: Yellow Flag or Yellow Triangle

Lexis and Westlaw assign yellow signals to cases that have not been reversed or overturned by a later case but have been cited in later cases in some negative manner. Lexis uses a yellow triangle and Westlaw uses a yellow flag to indicate negative treatment. Lexis uses an additional signal, a yellow box that contains a "Q," which is a stronger warning of possible negative treatment. The yellow signals have various meanings, some of which have little impact on the original case and some of which have significant impact on the original case. Similar to red signals, yellow signals suggest that the case must be carefully reviewed in order to determine the effect of the later case.

Yellow signals can indicate the following:

- A later court distinguishing a case from the original case because of different facts or different application of the law;
- A later court explicitly disagreeing with or criticizing the holding or reasoning of the original case;
- A later case limiting the application of the original case; or
- A later case questioning the continued validity of the original case.

Understanding the distinction between binding law and nonbinding law, especially in the context of the particular research question, is extremely important when using a citator. Signals will be assigned for negative treatment regardless of the jurisdiction or level of the court citing to the original case. For example, if a Connecticut Supreme Court case is assigned a yellow signal because a Supreme Court of Nebraska case distinguished its ruling, it has no practical effect on the Connecticut case. The ruling of the Supreme Court of Nebraska does not bind Connecticut courts, and it cannot affect the validity of a Connecticut Supreme Court case. Reviewing the Nebraska case may provide insight or further understanding of issues related to the case, but it will not affect the law of Connecticut.

3. Warning

There is a category of citator signals that are meant to warn that, although the original case has not been reversed or overruled, it may be in the future.

Overruling Risk

Lexis and Westlaw provide a warning when the original case relies on a case that has since been overturned by a later case. Because the later case does not directly cite the original case, a red signal is inaccurate. However, the warning signal indicates a weakness in the precedent of the original case, which should prompt further research to validate the law. Overruling risk is indicated by a box with the term "At Risk" on Shepard's and by an exclamation point within an orange circle on KeyCite.

Appealed to a Federal Court of Appeals

Westlaw assigns a blue striped flag to federal district court cases when they have been appealed to a federal court of appeals. Because the case will eventually be heard at the appellate level, it is possible that the case will be overturned on appeal, invalidating the district court case. Once the case is heard and decided at the federal court of appeals, the flag is removed.

4. Neutral

Neutral signals indicate that there are citing references for a case, but those references are neither positive nor negative. For example, the later case may provide an explanation or cite to the original case in order to show that earlier cases have decided the same issue. A neutral citing reference signal indicates that the original case remains valid. On Lexis, the neutral signal is an "A" within a blue hexagon; on Westlaw, the neutral signal is a green "C."

5. Positive

Only Shepard's provides a signal for positive treatment, which is a plus sign within a green diamond. The positive treatment signal means that a later case has followed or affirmed the original case. This signal should cause no concern regarding validity. This signal can be used as a research tool in that it points to later cases that affirmed the continued validity of the original case. If the original case is relevant to the research question, any cases marked with the positive treatment signal may lead to additional cases that strengthen the legal analysis.

C. Updating Statutes

Citators are also used to update statutes. Although changes to statutes are somewhat easier to follow due to the process required to amend them, Shepard's and KeyCite signals are still an efficient tool used to determine if a statute has been amended or may be amended.

A red signal—a red flag in KeyCite and an exclamation point within a red triangle in Shepard's—indicates that legislation has been enacted that will change the section.[2] A yellow signal—a yellow flag in KeyCite and an exclamation point in a yellow triangle in Shepard's—indicates that legislation is pending that would affect the statute if enacted.

In addition, citators signal when a court has determined that a statute or a part of a statute is unconstitutional. However, with those sources and signals, a researcher should not presume the entire statute is invalid. Courts may find a statute or a part of a statute unconstitutional only when applied to certain persons or in certain circumstances. Therefore, just as when using a citator with cases, it is important to carefully read the case and determine how it affects the validity of the statute in the context of the research question.

D. Citators as Research Tools

In addition to being validation tools, citators are helpful, effective, and efficient research tools. Because citators link documents through citation, they may be used to find additional relevant authority or explanatory material. Citators link all types of information, meaning that using a citator with a case will lead to later cases that cite the case, treatises, law review articles, and briefs filed in appellate cases. Reviewing treatises, law review articles, and other sources can provide a greater explanation of the case and its impact on the law. Chapter 7 provides additional information on using citators for case law research.

Using a citator with a statute results in a list of all cases that cite to that statute, which locates cases that apply and interpret the statute. Like with cases, a citator also points to any secondary sources that cites the statute. Chapter 4 provides additional information about using citators for statutory research.

---

2. There is usually a period of time between when a law is enacted and when it goes into effect. In Connecticut, legislation goes into effect on October 1 of the year it was passed unless the act specifies another date. Conn. Gen. Stat. § 2-32.

Chapter 10

An Introduction to Legal Citation

Legal citation plays a critical role in legal research and legal writing. Proper citation use substantiates the research, analyses, and legal writing at large, and it allows a reader to retrieve the authorities underlying the legal writing. This chapter addresses citation rules specific to the state of Connecticut; the two national citation manuals, *The Bluebook: A Uniform System of Citation* (21st ed.) ("*The Bluebook*")[1] and the *ALWD Guide to Legal Citation* (7th ed.) (the "*ALWD Guide*");[2] and the online, open-source, free content version of *The Bluebook* called *The Indigo Book: A Manual of Legal Citation* ("*The Indigo Book*").[3]

I. Purposes of Legal Citation

Mastering the proper use and form of legal citations will advance the credibility, efficiency, and overall quality of legal writing, as legal citation allows a writer to efficiently present a large amount of critical information, which is often derived from other authorities, to the reader.

A. Location

Citations allow a reader to find, consult, and further examine sources. Citations thus provide information necessary for a reader to validate a writer's claims and to potentially conduct further research.

---

1. Columbia L. Rev. Ass'n et al., eds., *The Bluebook: A Uniform System of Citation* (21st ed., Harvard Law Review Association 2020) [hereinafter *The Bluebook*].

2. Association of Legal Writing Directors & Carolyn V. Williams, *ALWD Guide to Legal Citation* (7th ed., Aspen Publishing 2021) [hereinafter *ALWD Guide*].

3. Christopher Jon Sprigman et al., *The Indigo Book: A Manual of Legal Citation* (Public.Resource.Org, Inc. 2016) [hereinafter *The Indigo Book*].

B. Citations to Judicial Opinions

The information contained in a citation instantly and efficiently tells a reader about the source and its importance to the legal analysis. For a judicial opinion, importance depends on whether the case is mandatory or persuasive precedent and, if the latter, its extent of persuasiveness. A judicial opinion's importance is therefore based on the following factors, all of which should be included in the citation: (1) jurisdiction of the deciding court; (2) level of the deciding court; (3) date of the decision; (4) relationship of the cited case to the text that it supports; (5) summary of the key part(s) of the decision; (6) validity of the case; and (7) any decisions in the same case that were made subsequent to the cited decision.

C. Citations to Legal Sources Other than Judicial Opinions

For legal sources other than judicial opinions, citations provide valuable information including the identity of authors, editors, and publishers; the date of the cited source; and the relationship between the cited source and the text.

II. When to Use Citations

Citations must be used whenever a writer refers to, depends on, builds on, or describes language or ideas that are not the writer's own. In other words, whenever a writer includes language or ideas from another source, a citation must attribute the language and/or ideas to their original source. Citations must be used in the following circumstances: (1) when the author describes a statute, regulation, case, article, book, speech, internet posting, or other source; (2) when the author includes, critiques, or expands on information from any source; and (3) when the author includes language directly quoted from any source.

III. Where to Place Citations

The proper placement of citations depends on the genre of legal writing in which the citation is included and the content of the citation. Citations may be placed within the text or in footnotes. Typically, for briefs and memoranda—documents commonly used in legal practice—citations are placed within the text. However, footnotes may also be used in these documents to address ancillary points or provide additional, less critical information. This practice is commonly referred to as "practitioner style," and it is addressed in the state and national citation manuals.

For articles and research papers—documents commonly used in academic settings—citations are placed within footnotes. This practice is commonly referred to as "law review style," and it is also addressed in the state and national citation manuals.

With both styles of citation, it is imperative that the in-text citation—as with practitioner style—or the footnote—as with law review style—be placed immediately after the material that it supports. Proper citation use may therefore require including a citation after a part of a sentence or after every sentence within a paragraph. When a writer omits a citation, they are claiming credit for the language and ideas contained in their legal writing.

IV. Legal Citation Manuals

There are state and national citation manuals, which are often available in print and online formats. A writer must adhere to the rules provided in the citation manuals in order to properly cite sources and properly place citations in their legal writing. A writer may find that in law practice, most firms, departments, and offices have their own citation style preferences. While it may seem like there are many rules and many sources to consult, the good news is that once practicing for a short amount of time, most lawyers memorize most of the relevant rules and can always refer to a manual for assistance.

A. Connecticut

A writer must be aware that there are state sources—including statutes, court rules, and manuals of style—that dictate the citation rules that must be adhered to before the courts of the specific state. In Connecticut, the source of citation rules is *The Manual of Style for the Connecticut Courts* ("*The Manual*").[4] *The Manual* provides the rules observed in the publication of opinions in the official reports of the state. It is "intended to assist all justices, judges, law clerks, and support staff" in order to achieve "relative consistency

4. *The Manual of Style for the Connecticut Courts* (3rd ed., The Office of the Reporter of Judicial Decisions 2013), https://www.jud.ct.gov/Publications/Manual_of_style.pdf [hereinafter *The Manual*].

of structure and format in the opinions published in the Connecticut Reports, Connecticut Appellate Reports, and Connecticut Supplement."[5] Table 10-1 depicts citations formatted in accordance with *The Manual.*

Table 10-1. Citations from *The Manual of Style for the Connecticut Courts*

Citations of State Sources from *The Manual of Style for the Connecticut Courts*	
Case	*State v. McKenzie-Adams,* 281 Conn. 486, 486, 915 A. 2d 822 (presumption in favor of joinder), cert. denied, 552 U.S. 888, 128 S. Ct. 248, 169 L. Ed. 2d 148 (2007).
Constitution	Conn. Const., art. 1, § 9.
Statute	General Statutes §§ 1-1, 1-2, 1-3 and 1-4.
Regulation	Regs. Conn. State Agencies § 13-142-211.

The Manual provides general style conventions and citation-specific style conventions. The general style conventions cover opinion organization, grammar, preferred usages, punctuation, capitalization, italicization, quotation, and more.[6] The citation-specific style conventions cover introductory signals, order of authorities, citation of primary and secondary authorities, citation of Connecticut sources, and more.[7] Though both the general style conventions and the citation-specific style conventions are important, the general style conventions may be more valuable in practice. The general style conventions—especially those on opinion organization[8] and on miscellaneous conventions and preferred usages[9]—tend to provide instruction that *The Bluebook* does not. The citation-specific style conventions, on the other hand, tend to provide instruction that *The Bluebook* does as well. In other words, the citation-specific conventions usually do not deviate from the conventions in *The Bluebook.* However, it is important to note that the citation-specific conventions in *The Manual* include examples that use Connecticut opinions, constitutions, statutes, public acts, special acts, and other state sources.

5. *Id.* at iv.
6. *See id.* at 1–53.
7. *See id.* at 54–106.
8. *See id.* at 1–14.
9. *See id.* at 19–28.

B. National Citation Manuals

There are two national citation manuals that provide instruction on the proper citation of various sources—*The Bluebook* and the *ALWD Guide*.

1. The Bluebook

The Bluebook is the uniform system of citation in the United States, providing "a systematic method by which members of the [legal] profession communicate important information about the sources and legal authorities upon which they rely in their work."[10] *The Bluebook* is organized into six parts: the Quick Reference Guides, the table of contents, the Bluepages, the Whitepages, the tables, and the index.

The Quick Reference Guides are printed inside the front cover and the back cover. The Quick Reference Guide printed inside the front cover is for citations in law review style. It provides examples of citations in the typeface required in law review footnotes, which are further explained in the Whitepages. The Quick Reference Guide printed inside the back cover is for citations in practitioner style. It provides examples of citations in the typeface required in court documents and legal memoranda, which are further explained in the Bluepages.

After the Quick Reference Guide printed inside the front cover, *The Bluebook* proceeds with a preface to the twenty-first edition detailing how some content, specifically some citation forms, have been "expanded, reduced, or modified from previous editions."[11] Then, it proceeds with a table of contents, which sets forth the structure of the manual, and an introduction, which covers the purpose, structure, and general principles of the manual and of citation, more generally.

The substance of *The Bluebook* begins with the Bluepages. The Bluepages, printed on blue paper, provide instruction based on practitioner style. The purpose of the section is to meet the basic citation needs of law students and practitioners who draft briefs, memoranda, and other legal documents. Following the Bluepages, the Whitepages, printed on white paper, provide instruction based on law review style. The Whitepages meet the more complex citation needs of those involved in the publication of scholarship in law reviews and law journals. As a result, the Whitepages are subdivided into

10. *The Bluebook*, *supra*, at 1.
11. *Id.* at vii.

two sections. The first section—Rules 1 through 9—establishes style and citation conventions for use in all forms of legal writing; the second section—Rules 10 through 21—establishes citation conventions for specific sources such as cases, statutes, and periodicals. It is important to note that the content of the Bluepages and the content of the Whitepages correspond. In other words, B10 in the Bluepages covers citation of cases, and Rule 10 in the Whitepages covers citation of cases as well. Following the Whitepages, the tables provide information to supplement all the conventions contained in the manual. For example, Table T1 provides the proper abbreviations of the U.S. jurisdictions; Table T1 is used in conjunction with B10 in the Bluepages, Rule 10 in the Whitepages, and several other citation forms that reference U.S. jurisdictions.

The Bluebook concludes with a comprehensive index. The index establishes a strong point of departure for the user; it allows the user to search for a key term(s) in order to locate the proper rule in the manual, which is over 350 pages in length.

2. The ALWD Guide

The *ALWD Guide*, published by the Association of Legal Writing Directors ("the ALWD"), explains citation in a pedagogical manner. The *ALWD Guide* is designed to assist users, such as law students, professors, judges, and other practitioners, in the practice of proper citation, whereas *The Bluebook* is not. However, the citations that result from use of the *ALWD Guide* are identical to the citations that result from use of *The Bluebook*.[12] The *ALWD Guide* provides Rule Correlation Guides, which evidence that the rules contained in the *ALWD Guide* are identical to the rules contained in *The Bluebook*.[13] But the ALWD has not yet released the Rule Correlation Guide that compares the current edition of the *ALWD Guide*, the seventh edition, to the current edition of *The Bluebook*, the twenty-first edition.

---

12. *FAQs*, A Publication of the Association of Legal Writing Directors: Guide to Legal Citation, https://www.alwd.org/guide-faqs (last visited July 4, 2021). Note that citations from earlier editions of the *ALWD Guide* were not identical to the citations from earlier editions of *The Bluebook*. The citation rules were made identical in the sixth edition of the *ALWD Guide*. *Id.*

13. *Rule Correlation Guides*, A Publication of the Association of Legal Writing Directors: Guide to Legal Citation, https://www.alwd.org/guide-rule-correlation-guides (last visited July 4, 2021).

The *ALWD Guide* is organized into six parts. Part 1, "Citation Basics," introduces the basic concepts used to cite sources, including full citations, short citations, abbreviations, pinpoint references, and more. Part 2, "Citing Specific Sources," provides citation formats for primary authorities and secondary authorities, both print and electronic, that are most often used in legal writing. Part 3, "Online Sources," provides citations formats for the electronic sources that are not addressed in Part 2. Such online sources include sources available on the internet, on commercial databases, and on blogs. Part 4, "Incorporating Citations into Documents," exhibits the placement of citations in text, including citation clauses, citation sentences, embedded citations, and citations in academic footnotes. In addition, Part 4 exhibits the proper use of signals and parentheticals. Part 5, "Quotations," explains proper incorporation of quotations into legal documents, alterations in quotations, and omissions from quotations. Finally, Part 6, "Appendices," collects information for constructing legal citations, including general and specialized abbreviations for official and unofficial reporters, statutes, administrative publications, and legal periodicals.

3. The Indigo Book

The Indigo Book is an open implementation of the uniform system of citation provided in *The Bluebook*. *The Indigo Book* is not the same as *The Bluebook*; however, it is compatible with the twentieth edition of *The Bluebook*. Its content is similar to the content of the Bluepages, as it allows for proper citation of sources in briefs, memoranda, articles, and other legal documents. Though *The Indigo Book* is not the principal citation manual, it is free of charge to users, and it is free of copyright restrictions, meaning that it may be distributed in its HTML or PDF format to law students, practitioners, and others interested in the information that it provides.[14]

V. Citation Components and Format

Because *The Bluebook* provides the uniform system of citation in the United States, the following explanations of citations are based on the rules set forth in *The Bluebook*. However, because the *ALWD Guide* is frequently used and its rules are identical to those of *The Bluebook*, the following explanations of citations are based on the *ALWD Guide* as well. But, as mentioned,

---

14. *The Indigo Book*, *supra*, at Introduction.

the ALWD has not yet released the Rule Correlation Guide that compares the current edition of the *ALWD Guide*, the seventh edition, to the current edition of *The Bluebook*, the twenty-first edition.

A. Case Citations

Under Rule 10 of *The Bluebook* and Rule 12 of *The ALWD Guide*, a complete citation of a case includes: the name of the case, the volume and the reporter in which the case is published, the first page of the case, the specific page or page range that contains the information being cited (i.e., the pinpoint citation), the deciding court, and the date on which the case was decided. Depending on the case, a complete citation may also include the prior and subsequent history of the case. Below are examples of complete citations of a Connecticut Appellate Court case and a Connecticut Supreme Court case, with and without parallel citations, which were composed in accordance with Rule 10 of *The Bluebook* and Rule 12 of the *ALWD Guide*:

Table 10-2. Connecticut Appellate Court Case Citation

See	Connecticut Coal. for Just. in Educ. Funding, Inc.	v. Rell	, 176	A.3d	28	, 35	(Conn.	2018).
1	2	3	4	5	6	7	8	9

1	Introductory signal
2	First party
3	Second party
4	Reporter volume number
5	Reporter abbreviation (Atlantic Reporter)
6	First page of case
7	Specific page referred to
8	Deciding court
9	Year of decision

Table 10-3. Connecticut Supreme Court Case Citation With and Without Parallel Citations

Case Citation With and Without Parallel Citations	
With Parallel Citations:	*Connecticut Coal. for Just. in Educ. Funding, Inc. v. Rell*, 327 Conn. 650, 650, 176 A.3d 28, 28 (2018).
Without Parallel Citations	*Connecticut Coal. for Just. in Educ. Funding, Inc. v. Rell*, 176 A.3d 28, 28 (Conn. 2018).

The citations provided in Table 10-2 and Table 10-3 adhere to the practitioner style. Remember that the name of the case should be italicized or underlined if adhering to the practitioner style, but it should not be italicized, underlined, or otherwise modified if adhering to the law review style.

As mentioned, a complete citation of a case includes several components. Table 10-4 depicts a sample citation with its components.

Table 10-4. Connecticut Supreme Court Case Citation

See	*Connecticut Coal. for Just. in Educ. Funding, Inc.*	*v.*	*Rell*	,	176	A.3d	28	,	35	(Conn.	2018).
1	2	v.	3		4	5	6		7	8	9

Case Citation Components

1	Introductory signal
2	First party
3	Second party
4	Reporter volume number
5	Reporter abbreviation (*Atlantic Reporter, 3d*)
6	First page of case
7	Pinpoint citation
8	Deciding court
9	Year of decision

The first component is the introductory signal. Signals organize authorities and indicate how those authorities support or relate to a proposition in the text. Citation sentences may contain more than one signal. Signals are governed by Rules 1.2, 1.3, and 1.4 of *The Bluebook* and by Rules 35 and 36 of the *ALWD Guide*.

The second and third components are found in the name of the case, which may be in normal typeface, italicized, or underlined, depending on the style (practitioner style or law review style) and the placement of the citation (in a footnote or in the text). Use the name that appears at the beginning of the decision in the cited reporter. The name of the case is governed by Rule 10.2 of *The Bluebook* and by Rule 12.2 of the *ALWD Guide*. Omit all parties other than the first party listed on each side of the "v." Abbreviate the remaining parties and any procedural phrases according to Rule 10.2.2 of *The Bluebook* and Rule 12.2, specifically Rule 12.2(b)–(r), of the *ALWD Guide*. After the name of the case, insert a comma. The comma should never be italicized, underlined, or otherwise modified.

The fourth and fifth components, respectively, are the volume and the reporter in which the case is published. The reporter is governed by Rule 10.3 of *The Bluebook*, which requires that the reporter be abbreviated according to the rule and Table T1, which indicates the reporters that contain most decisions. Alternatively, the volume and the reporter are governed by Rules 12.3 and 12.4 of the *ALWD Guide*. The reporter must be abbreviated according to Rule 12.4(a).

The sixth component is the first page of the case, followed by a comma. The seventh component is the page or page range that contains the information being cited, which is known as the pinpoint citation. If the information being cited is on the first page of the case, then the page number must appear twice, separated by the necessary comma. The use of page numbers is exhibited in the example that begins Rule 10 of *The Bluebook*, but it is explicitly governed by Rule 12.5 of the *ALWD Guide*.

The eighth and ninth components are included in the same parenthetical. The eighth component is the deciding court, which must be abbreviated according to Rule 10.4 of *The Bluebook*, which ultimately directs the user to Tables T1, T2, T7, or T10. Alternatively, it must be abbreviated according to Rule 12.6 of the *ALWD Guide*. However, if the reporter clearly indicates the deciding court, then the deciding court does not need to be stated in the parenthetical. The ninth component is the exact date or year of the case. The exact date must be provided for unreported cases and for cases cited in slip opinions, electronic databases, or other sources listed in Rule 10.5(b) of *The Bluebook*. For pending cases and cases dismissed without opinion, the exact date or year of the most recent major disposition must be provided. Date or year are governed by Rule 10.5 of *The Bluebook* and by Rule 12.7 of the *ALWD Guide*.

An additional component is the prior and subsequent history of the case. Unlike the other components, the additional component is not required in all case citations, according to Rule 10.7 of *The Bluebook* and Rules 12.8, 12.9, and 12.10 of the *ALWD Guide*. Typically, the prior history is required only if it is significant to the point for which the case is cited, and the subsequent history is required only if it is significant to the point for which the case is cited or if the decision is cited in full.

A citation typically ends with a period. However, there are some exceptions. A citation may end with a comma if it is placed within a sentence. Consider a sentence that is composed of two independent clauses. The first independent clause requires Citation 1, and the second independent clause requires Citation 2. Citation 1 must immediately follow the first independent clause, so Citation 1 must be set off from the rest of the sentence with a pair of commas. Citation 2 must immediately follow the second independent clause, but Citation 2 must be placed in its own citation sentence. That is, it must constitute its own sentence, as a normal citation would.

Another exception is permitted if multiple citations follow one signal. All but the final citation end with semicolons. The final citation ends with a period.

B. Constitution Citations

Under Rule 11 of *The Bluebook* and Rule 13 of the *ALWD Guide*, a complete citation of the U.S. Constitution includes the abbreviation "U.S." and the word "Const." *The Bluebook* requires that the word "CONST." appears in large and small capital letters, whereas the *ALWD Guide* does not. Under the same rule of *The Bluebook*, a complete citation of a state constitution includes the abbreviation of the state according to Table T10 and the word "CONST." in large and small capital letters. The *ALWD Guide* requires the same, although the abbreviation of the state is made according to Appendix 3(B) and the word "Const." appears in regular typeface. A complete citation also includes the abbreviation of the subdivisions of the constitution, such as articles and clauses. Below are citations of the U.S. Constitution and the Constitution of the State of Connecticut according to Rule 11 of *The Bluebook*. Note that the structure of the citations would be the same according to Rule 13 of the *ALWD Guide*, but the citations would be in regular typeface, rather than large and small capital letters.

- U.S. Const. art. I, § 2.
- Conn. Const. art. IV, § 2, cl. 2.

C. Statute Citations

Under Rule 12 of *The Bluebook* and Rule 14 of the *ALWD Guide*, a citation of a federal statute or a provision of a federal statute should be made to the *United States Code* (U.S.C.), the current official code, when applicable. Under both *The Bluebook* and the *ALWD Guide*, a complete citation of a federal statute in U.S.C. includes (1) the title number, (2) the code abbreviation, (3) the section number, (4) the publisher (except for U.S.C.), and (5) the date of the hardbound volume in which the statute is published. It is important to note that the fifth component is optional under *The Bluebook*. Below is a citation of a provision of the *United States Code*:

- 38 U.S.C. §§ 1968–1970.

A citation to the *Connecticut General Statutes* and other state statutes includes the same components as a citation to the *United States Code*. Below is a citation of a provision of the *Connecticut General Statutes*:

- Conn. Gen. Stat. § 10-15h (2012).

D. Regulation Citations

Under Rule 14 of *The Bluebook* and Rule 18 of the *ALWD Guide*, a citation of a federal regulation or a provision of a federal regulation should be made to the *Code of Federal Regulations* (C.F.R.), when applicable. Under both *The Bluebook* and the *ALWD Guide*, a complete citation of a federal regulation in C.F.R. includes (1) the title, (2) the section or part, and (3) the year. Each title of C.F.R. is revised at least once a year, so a citation must be made to the most recent edition. If a federal regulation has not yet been codified in C.F.R., then a citation should be made to the *Federal Register* (Fed. Reg.), which publishes rules and regulations before they are entered into C.F.R. A complete citation of a federal rule or regulation in Fed. Reg. includes (1) the commonly used name of the rule or regulation, (2) the volume and page on which the rule, regulation, or any preceding discussion thereof begins, and (3) the date of the rule or regulation. A complete citation of a provision of a federal rule or regulation in Fed. Reg. includes (1) the page on which the rule, regulation, or any preceding discussion thereof begins, (2) the page(s) on which the cited material appears, and (3) a parenthetical indicating where the rule or regulation will appear when codified in C.F.R. Below are citations to a provision of C.F.R. and a provision of Fed. Reg.:

- 7 C.F.R. § 319.76 (2019).
- Importation of Fruits and Vegetables, 60 Fed. Reg. 50,379, 50,381 (Sept. 29, 1995) (to be codified at 7 C.F.R. pts. 300, 319).

A citation to a Connecticut rule or regulation and other state rules or regulations should be made in accordance with the federal examples provided in Rule 14 of *The Bluebook* and Rule 18 of the *ALWD Guide*. Below is a citation of a provision of a Connecticut regulation:

- Conn. Agencies Regs. § 19-13-B42 (2019).

Chapter 11

An Introduction to Legal Writing

Results of legal research must be synthesized, applied to the research question, and communicated to a specific audience in an appropriate tone. Legal writing is the medium used to explain the results of legal research and the applicability of the results. There are several types or genres of legal writing—persuasive, predictive, and executory. Regardless of genre, effective legal writing requires logical organization, clear and concise style, and strict attribution of credit to sources.

I. Genres of Legal Writing

There are several types or genres of legal writing. They vary in style, perspective, goal, and intended audience. Table 11-1 describes the genres and their key distinguishing features.

Table 11-1. Genres of Legal Writing

Genres of Legal Writing		
Persuasive Writing	Predictive Writing	Executory Writing
Examples Briefs, demand letters, negotiation letters, etc.	Examples Legal memoranda, email memoranda, client letters, etc.	Examples Statutes, wills, contracts, etc.
Perspective Subjective	Perspective Objective	Perspective Future Tense

(continued on next page)

Goal To advocate a position to the reader	Goal To predict an outcome, without arguing for a particular one	Goal To prescribe rules to govern future conduct
Intended Audience Courts, tribunals, and opposing parties when motivating a concession, compliance, or transaction	Intended Audience Other lawyers and clients	Intended Audience Parties imposing rules that govern future conduct and parties subject to rules that govern future conduct

A. Persuasive Writing

Persuasive writing seeks to advocate. It seeks to convince the reader of the accuracy of a position and the need to take certain action. As a result, persuasive writing is often considered to be subjective because the writer advances a particular position, purpose, or goal. Persuasive writing is the type of writing that most people envision lawyers and other members of the legal profession doing.

The key components of persuasive writing include an introductory statement that identifies the action or relief sought; an accurate, interesting, credible, and persuasive description of relevant facts, supported by citations to the sources in which the facts were found; a persuasive explanation of the relevant law and application of the law to the operative facts; and a conclusion that reminds the reader of what the author seeks and the supporting reasons. Table 11-2 depicts the main components of persuasive writing.

Table 11-2. Components of Persuasive Writing

Components of Persuasive Writing
Introductory statement that identifies the action or relief sought
Persuasive description of the relevant facts, supported by proper citations
Persuasive explanation of the relevant law and its application to the relevant facts
Conclusion that affirms the action or relief sought and the supporting law

In persuasive writing, it is important to consider potential arguments that could be made against the author's position. While it might seem counterintuitive, admitting and responding to potential opposing arguments will enhance the credibility and persuasion of the writing. Therefore, in conducting legal research, a researcher should always take note of authorities that may support potential opposing arguments.

In the legal profession, examples of persuasive writing include briefs—written arguments submitted to convince courts or other tribunals—and demand or negotiation letters—letters written on a client's behalf to motivate a concession, compliance, or transaction.

B. Predictive Writing

Predictive writing seeks to educate. It seeks to deliver an objective explanation or analysis to the reader. It is neutral in tone because the author's goal is to clearly and objectively predict an outcome, without arguing for a result. Predictive writing often occurs earlier in the lawyering process than persuasive writing because it is used when lawyers educate one another and their clients about the law and its impact on a given case.

The key components of predictive writing include a statement that introduces the issue; an overview of the predictive conclusion; an objective description of the relevant facts; an explanation of the relevant law and application of the law to the operative facts; and a conclusion that reminds the reader of the likely outcome and any recommendations for further action, consideration, or analysis. Table 11-3 depicts the main components of predictive writing.

Table 11-3. Components of Predictive Writing

Components of Predictive Writing
Introductory statement that identifies the issue
Overview of the predictive conclusion
Objective descripton of the relevant facts, supported by proper citations
Objective explanation of the relevant law and its application to the relevant facts
Conclusion that affirms the predictive conclusion and recommendations for further action, consideration, or analysis

In predictive writing, it is important to be neutral and objective. An author should not advocate for a particular outcome; the description of relevant facts and the relevant law should not be impacted by a desired outcome. Instead, an author should use predictive writing as the means to identify weaknesses in a case. After all, a client would rather be alerted to weaknesses before pursuing a case, expending resources, and later learning that the case had significant weaknesses and risks.

An author should consider weaknesses, strengths, and the likely outcome of a case throughout the processes of legal research and legal writing. Readers will often ask for an estimated likelihood of the author's prediction, so it is important to consider the language used to convey probability. Therefore, when conducting legal research, the author should take note of the strength of support for each position. The strength of support depends on the jurisdiction, level, similarity, and specificity of the court opinions and other authorities identified during legal research.

In the legal profession, examples of predictive writing include legal memoranda comprised of written explanations, analyses, and predictions; email memoranda comprised of abbreviated explanations, analyses, and predictions; and client letters, comprised of communications to clients that seek to educate them and predict outcomes of their respective cases.

C. Executory Writing

Executory writing seeks to prescribe rules to govern future conduct. Executory writing is seldom labeled as such, although it appears throughout the legal profession. Executory writing anticipates and addresses matters that are yet to be fully performed, and it constructs rules to apply to future conduct.

The key components of executory writing include a clear definition of the parties and conduct that will be subject to its terms; required conduct, payment, or performance; prohibited conduct or performance; consequences of violating its terms; and methods of enforcing its terms and resolving disputes about them. Table 11-4 depicts the main components of executory writing.

Table 11-4. Components of Executory Writing

Components of Executory Writing
Introductory statement that identifies the parties and the conduct that will be subject to its terms
Statement that identifies the required conduct, payment, or performance
Statement that identifies the prohibited conduct or performance
Explanation of the consequences of violating the terms
Explanation of the methods of enforcing the terms and resolving disputers about the terms

In executory writing, it is important to consider all the potential conduct that could be regulated and to decide which conduct to regulate through clear provisions that will guide the parties and others who must review the provisions to resolve a dispute. The appropriate style for executory writing is clear, concise, and appropriate for the subject matter.

Examples of executory writing include wills, statutes, and contracts—documents that create rules that will govern future conduct. Drafting these documents requires an understanding of the law, including existing requirements and interpretations of certain provisions by courts. Therefore, before drafting, an author should research the relevant law and consult model documents or forms.

II. Organization of Legal Writing

Like legal research, legal writing must be well organized. There are several models for organizing legal writing, but all seek to achieve one purpose: to clarify the analysis or argument by providing a thorough explanation of the law before applying it to the relevant facts. For simplicity, this book will introduce the TRAC model, although variations exist such as IRAC and CRAC. TRAC, IRAC, and CRAC are acronyms for models of organizing legal writing, which have been created and taught by professors and textbook authors to facilitate learning of legal writing. Each model achieves the same purpose and will improve the organization and clarity of the legal analysis, argument, and writing.

A. Legal Writing in a Common Law System

In the United States, laws derive from constitutions, statutes, regulations, and judicial opinions on both the federal and state levels. Where these primary sources do not provide binding law within a jurisdiction, primary sources outside of the jurisdiction and/or secondary sources of law may provide persuasive authority. Consequently, explaining the law in a common law system may be especially complex. It is therefore essential to use a model for organizing legal writing that clearly explains the law to the reader before discussing how the law applies to the relevant facts.

B. TRAC, IRAC, CRAC, and More

TRAC is an acronym for Thesis, Rule, Application, and Conclusion. IRAC is an acronym for Issue, Rule, Application, and Conclusion. CRAC is an acronym for Conclusion, Rule, Application, and Conclusion. There are other models and associated acronyms that are used in legal writing, so an author should be prepared to adapt to the model preferred by a professor or employer.

In any piece of quality legal writing, the components of the TRAC, IRAC, or CRAC paradigms should be recognizable. In persuasive briefs, predictive memoranda, and judicial opinions, an author should separate their discussion of the law from their discussion of the relevant facts. The same approach is apparent in oral arguments: first, the law student or lawyer explains the law; then they apply it to the relevant facts. Table 11-5 depicts the structure of the TRAC model, and it briefly explains each part of the model.

Table 11-5. Structure of TRAC Model

TRAC
Thesis or Topic Statement that identifies the thesis or topic of the legal writing
Rule Statement that explains the relevant law that governs the issue in the legal writing (rule statement), supported by an analysis of the supporting sources (rule proof)
Application Application of the rule to the relevant facts of the given matter, mainly done through the processes of comparing and contrasting
Conclusion Statement that affirms the thesis and the supporting reasoning

C. One TRAC for Each Legal Issue

Within a legal document, one TRAC should be used to analyze each legal issue. For example, if the legal issue is application of a statute, then the author must provide a TRAC for each component of the statute. In other words, if the statute has three requirements, then the author must provide three TRACs. Where there are multiple TRACs, the author must address the relationship between them. The author should inform the reader of whether each legal issue must be satisfied or resolved or whether only one must be. Are the legal issues cumulative requirements or alternative requirements? A reader should understand how each legal issue—and therefore each TRAC—relates to the others and to the entire issue facing the client. Table 11-6 depicts the structure of the TRAC model when there is an overarching thesis and an overarching conclusion, but multiple subtheses, subrules, subapplications, and subconclusions.

Table 11-6. Structure of Multiple TRACs

Structure of Multiple TRACS
Overall Thesis
Overall Rule
Sub-TRAC 1: Thesis
Sub-TRAC 1: Rule
Sub-TRAC 1: Application
Sub-TRAC 1: Conclusion
Sub-TRAC 2: Thesis
Sub-TRAC 2: Rule
Sub-TRAC 2: Application
Sub-TRAC 2: Conclusion
Overall Application
Overall Concluson

D. Persuasive or Predictive Writing

An author should use TRAC or a similar model for organizing legal writing. TRAC is preferrable when writing persuasive briefs, predictive memoranda, and essay exam answers. TRAC is also preferrable when making oral presentations and oral arguments.

E. The TRAC Model

Because the concepts expressed in legal writing are often complex, it is important to use a clear model to organize legal writing and guide the reader through the legal analysis. While the models share similar components, this book focuses on TRAC. One distinguishing and advantageous feature of TRAC is that the author begins each analysis by stating a conclusion—a thesis—so that the reader immediately learns the author's request or prediction.

1. Thesis or Topic

Each TRAC begins with a clear statement of the thesis or legal issue. In persuasive writing, a TRAC begins with a thesis—one or two sentences that identify the outcome sought and the supporting reason(s) that the reader (a court) should grant relief in the lawyer's favor. A persuasive thesis is commonly formulated to state: "The Court should . . . because . . . ."

In predictive writing, a TRAC begins with a thesis—one or two sentences that explain a prediction and the supporting reason(s). A predictive thesis is commonly formulated to state: "It is likely that a court will . . . because . . . ." In predictive writing, a TRAC may also begin with a topic sentence that identifies the issue that will be analyzed. An example of this type of topic sentence is: "The issue in the case at bar is whether . . . .

2. Rule and Rule Proof

The second part of a TRAC—rule statement and rule proof—synthesizes and explains the law to the reader.

A rule statement is an affirmative statement of the law that the author asserts governs the issue at the core of the legal writing. The rule statement should synthesize the results of the research. The rule statement may therefore be based on a statute, case, combination of the two, and/or other sources, and it should be supported by citations to relevant authorities.

After the rule statement, the author must provide the rule proof, which explains the supporting law, especially primary sources such as cases. In this section, it is also important to explain how the sources relate to one another. These relationships are called "syntheses," and they assist the reader in understanding the sources, their relationships, and their implications in a larger legal context. For example, one case may expand on a prior case's holding or create an exception to it. By synthesizing the sources and explaining the same to the reader, the author performs intense analytical work and provides a clear explanation of the law.

3. Application

The third part of a TRAC—application—applies the law to the facts of a problem through the processes of comparing and contrasting. This part explains the similarities or analogies between the law and the facts, as well as the differences or distinctions between them. Reliance on precedent, or *stare decisis*, will drive the outcome if there are more similarities. But where there are more differences, the court may not follow precedent. For this reason, in the application part of TRAC, it is important to address positions that oppose the outcome that the author advocates or the prediction that the author explains.

4. *Conclusion*

The last part of a TRAC—conclusion—repeats the author's thesis—the statement of the outcome that the author seeks or the prediction that the author makes, as well as the supporting reasoning.

III. Style, Grammar, and Punctuation

Strong legal writing is characterized by a clear and concise style that guides the reader through the legal analysis with efficiency. The author's guiding principle should be to provide information that the reader needs or wants, rather than to provide information in which the author is interested.

The following are essential techniques to use in legal writing.

- Use clear prose so that the reader may focus on the substance of the legal writing, rather than its form.
- Do not write from the first-person perspective. Objectively state the decision or outcome that the precedent or other sources support.
- Write about cases in the past tense. Similarly, write about the facts and procedure of the given case in the past tense. However, write about the sought decision or outcome of the given case in the present tense.
- Refer to courts, corporations, and other entities with the pronoun "it." Refer to members of these entities with the pronoun "they."
- Place punctuation that is included in the source inside of quotation marks. Place punctuation that is not included in the source inside or outside of quotation marks, depending on the structure of the sentence. Use commas to set off introductory phrases, to join independent clauses with a coordinating conjunction, to separate items in a list, or to introduce quotations. Use semicolons to join independent clauses without a coordinating conjunction or to separate complex items in a list.
- State ideas directly, concisely, and without unnecessary introductory phrases. For example, a phrase like "it must be remembered that" does not add value to a sentence. Adverbs like "clearly" and "obviously" should not be used.

- Use specific nouns and active verbs instead of vague nouns and passive verbs. These words and phrases will make writing clearer, more concise, and interesting. For example, a vague, passive phrase stating that "the premises were repaired" could be replaced with a specific, active phrase stating that "the landlord repaired the premises."
- Ensure that subjects and verbs agree. Subjects and verbs should be close to each other in sentences, as should objects and verbs.
- Strive to use the most clear, concise, and vivid language. For example, write "the parties agreed" instead of "the parties decided to enter the agreement."
- Construct distinct paragraphs for distinct topics. Separate large or complicated topics into distinct subtopics and construct separate paragraphs for each. Use the TRAC model for each topic. Transition from paragraph to paragraph with phrases or sentences that show how the topics relate to each other.
- Use thesis sentences, transitional phrases, and transitional sentences to logically proceed between paragraphs and the writing at large.
- Do not include contractions, rhetorical questions, conversational terms, sexist wording, or informal or inappropriate abbreviations. Legal writing is formal, although it should not include lawyerly language that is too complicated for the matter. Use simple, direct sentence structure and language that the reader will understand without issue.

IV. Plagiarism

Legal writing demands thorough and detailed citation to sources that account for language or ideas that do not originate from the author themself. The requirement of citations is one of honesty (to show the reader when the author borrows or builds on another's work), diligence (to demonstrate the author's research), and attribution (to credit others when the author uses their intellectual property).

A. What Is Plagiarism?

Plagiarism occurs when a legal writer fails to include quotations or citations, thus failing to attribute credit to the proper sources.

If an author does not include attribution immediately after language or ideas, they are assuring the reader that the specific content originates from them. If an author is unsure of whether to include attribution, the author should ask a professor or employer for guidance before submitting work. Upon submitting work, the author represents that any material not supported by citations is their own. If this is not correct, then the author has committed plagiarism, regardless of their intent.

Plagiarism is a dire flaw in the quality of legal writing and a legal writer's reputation. If the author plagiarizes, whether intentionally or unintentionally, their academic and professional integrity will suffer. Plagiarism may jeopardize and forever mar their performance in a course, their eligibility for a degree or a professional license, and their professional reputation.

B. How to Avoid Plagiarism

An author will avoid plagiarism if they appropriately cite to sources of language and ideas that do not originate from them. Chapter 10 provides a detailed explanation of legal citation. The best method for avoiding plagiarism is taking scrupulous care during research and writing in order to attribute all material to its proper source. Keeping material and source attributions together throughout the research and writing process will help the author avoid accidentally omitting attribution or forgetting which source supports a point.

Another important method for avoiding plagiarism is conducting thorough research to become familiar with all material on the topic so that an author does not inadvertently write about another author's ideas without attribution.

Chapter 12

Court Rules and Legal Ethics

I. Court Rules

A. Introduction

Court rules govern practice before state and federal courts. Court rules cover pleadings, motions, discovery, trials, and all other procedural matters in all cases. Court rules may apply to all cases in a particular court; apply to only certain types of cases, such as criminal cases; or apply to certain subdivisions of a court, such as a geographical subdivision. When researching court rules, it is important to identify and consider all rules that apply to a case.

B. Connecticut Court Rules

Rules governing Connecticut courts are published in the *Connecticut Practice Book* (the "*Practice Book*"). The *Practice Book* contains the Rules of Professional Conduct, the Code of Judicial Conduct, the Rules for the Superior Court, and the Rules of Appellate Procedure. The Rules for the Superior Court include rules for civil, criminal, family, and juvenile matters. The Rules of Appellate Procedure apply to both the appellate court and the supreme court. The Probate Court Rules of Procedure are not published in the *Practice Book* and instead are published separately.

In addition to the rules in the *Practice Book*, courts issue *standing orders*, which are orders related to practice before a specific court that typically cover technical details such as scheduling or rules for special dockets, such as the Child Protection Docket. The *Practice Book* and standing orders are freely available on the Connecticut judicial branch website, and the *Practice Book* is also available in print.[1]

The *Practice Book* is republished every year, incorporating recent amendments to the rules. The amendments to the rules have different origins. The judicial branch Committee on Superior Court Rules creates and amends the Rules for the Superior Court. The justices of the appellate court and the supreme court create and amend the Rules of Appellate Procedure. Proposed rules are available on the Connecticut judicial branch website, and notices of new rules in the *Practice Book* are published in the *Connecticut Law Journal*.

C. Federal Court Rules

Federal courts are governed by the Federal Rules of Civil Procedure, the Federal Rules of Criminal Procedure, and the Federal Rules of Appellate Procedure. Each circuit of the federal courts of appeals is governed by its own rules, and each federal district court is governed by its local rules. These rules are often technical in nature, covering the formats of documents, methods of filing documents, schedules, motion practices, and the like. Federal court rules are published as appendices to the *United States Code*. Local rules are freely available on the website of each federal district court. Similar to federal courts, specialized courts, such as the bankruptcy court and the court of federal claims, and individual courts are governed by their own supplemental rules.

D. Annotated Court Rules

Research into court rules is most easily accomplished through annotated rules. Official rules provide the text of the rule, but annotated rules include references to cases that demonstrate how the rule is applied under various sets of facts. Annotations are organized by topic, which may help locate cases on various subtopics that involve application of the rule.

Annotated statutes include annotated court rules, and both are available in print, on Lexis, and on Westlaw. Westlaw also publishes annotated court rules that are specifically for practice in Connecticut state and federal courts.[2]

---

1. *Connecticut Practice Book*, https://www.jud.ct.gov/publications/PracticeBook/PB.pdf.

2. *West's Connecticut Rules of Court Annotated* includes the Superior Court Rules, Connecticut Rules of Appellate Procedure, Appendix of Forms, Code of Evidence, Code of Judicial Conduct, Rules of Professional Conduct, Statewide

Though court rules are available online, they are often referenced in print. Browsing and reviewing various rules is faster using a print book, especially considering that local rules and standing orders must be reviewed in conjunction with court rules.

The statutory research techniques described in chapter 4 may be applied to court rules. Court rules can be located through statutory indexes, browsed in the statutory code's table of contents, and keyword searched in electronic databases.

E. Rules Treatises

Rules treatises are even more in-depth resources for research into court rules. In addition to case annotations, rules treatises provide explanations, analyses, and histories of court rules. Rules treatises are organized to reflect the organization of court rules, and they include extensive subject indexes. Thus, information can be accessed by the court rule number or by the subject through the index.

The *Connecticut Practice Series Superior Court Civil Rules*[3] provides the most in-depth analysis of civil rules in the *Practice Book*. In this publication, each rule is accompanied by a substantial explanation of how the rule has been applied with citations to relevant cases. The *Connecticut Practice Series Superior Court Civil Rules* also includes similar volumes on criminal procedure and appellate procedure.

Moore's Federal Practice[4] and *Wright & Miller Federal Practice and Procedure*[5] are the two major rules treatises for practice in federal court. These treatises provide information about the historical development and current application of the rules in federal court.

Grievance Committee Rules of Procedure, Probate Court Rules and Procedure, and Superior Court Standing Orders.

3. Wesley W. Horton & Kimberly A. Knox, *Connecticut Practice Series: Superior Court Civil Rules* (Thomson West 2004).

4. James William Moore & Daniel R. Coquillette, *Moore's Federal Practice* (Matthew Bender 1997) (available on Westlaw).

5. Arthur R. Miller et al., *Federal Practice and Procedure* (Thomson West 1969) (available on Westlaw).

II. Legal Ethics and Rules of Professional Conduct

A. Rules of Professional Conduct

The Rules of Professional Conduct govern the ethical conduct of lawyers admitted to practice in Connecticut courts. The rules cover confidentiality, use of client funds, conduct before the court, and other mandates related to legal practice. Lawyers, therefore, must be familiar with the rules and comply with them. In addition to the Rules of Professional Conduct, there are sources of guidance in the form of disciplinary decisions and advisory ethics opinions. Research into these decisions and opinions may provide insight into how the rules apply under various sets of facts.

The Rules of Professional Conduct are published in the *Practice Book* and contain the text of the rule and significant commentary on the terminology in the rule. The Rules of Professional Conduct are on Lexis and Westlaw, where, like statutes, they include Notes of Decision and access to citing references.

B. The Statewide Grievance Committee

Attorney conduct in Connecticut is regulated by the Statewide Grievance Committee, which hears disciplinary complaints made against lawyers and issues written decisions. These decisions, available on the Statewide Grievance Committee website, provide information on how the Rules of Professional Conduct are applied when determining whether a lawyer has engaged in misconduct.[6] These decisions are extensively indexed by date, party name, case number, subject, and Rule of Professional Conduct. Therefore, although the decisions are not accessible by keyword search, it is possible to locate decisions regarding a specific issue of misconduct.

Decisions of the Statewide Grievance Committee are appealed to the superior court. Court decisions related to Rules of Professional Conduct may be easily found using a citator for the specific rule in Lexis or Westlaw.

---

6. Statewide Grievance Committee Decisions, https://jud.ct.gov/sgcdecisions/.

C. Ethics Opinions

Following an ethical course of behavior is not always a clear path for lawyers. In the variety of situations that may occur during legal practice, lawyers will not always know the correct conduct under the Rules of Professional Conduct. The Connecticut Bar Association (CBA) provides opinions on questions of ethics to assist lawyers with compliance. Unlike bar associations in some other states, the CBA is strictly a professional organization, and it does not regulate or discipline attorneys. Nevertheless, the CBA's ethical opinions hold persuasive weight in Connecticut courts, and they can be a source of information for lawyers evaluating their own conduct.

The CBA Committee on Professional Responsibility responds to ethical questions of its members by issuing formal opinions and informal opinions. Formal opinions are issued infrequently and only when the committee determines that the question is one of significant importance to the entire bar. Informal opinions are issued more frequently, but they are only issued in response to an individual lawyer's question. Both types of opinions are made available by the CBA on the CBA website, Lexis, Westlaw, and in the *Professional Responsibility Reference Guide*, a publication of the CBA.[7]

D. Other Sources for Legal Ethics Research

For further research into legal ethics, *Connecticut Legal Ethics and Malpractice* provides analyses of the Rules of Professional Conduct and lawyers' ethical obligations.[8] For more research into legal ethics or into issues that the Connecticut rules do not address, the American Bar Association Model Rules of Professional Conduct (MRPC) and ethics decisions in other states may provide guidance. The MRPC may be adopted by states in whole or in part. Consequently, many states have very similar ethical rules, the application of which may provide insight into issues that have not yet been addressed in Connecticut.

Similarly, the *ABA/BNA Lawyers Manual on Professional Responsibility* may be used as a source for ethical research, as it provides analyses of the

7. Connecticut Bar Association Committee on Professional Ethics, *Professional Responsibility Reference Guide* (Connecticut Bar Association 1993).

8. Mark A. Dubois & James F. Sullivan, *Connecticut Legal Ethics and Malpractice* (3rd ed., Connecticut Law Tribune 2016).

MRPC, practice guides for major areas of professional responsibility, ethics opinions from different jurisdictions, and news services.[9] Other major secondary sources for ethical research include *The Law of Lawyering* and *The Restatement (Third) of the Law Governing Lawyers.*[10]

---

9. The *ABA/BNA Manual on Professional Responsibility* is available only on Bloomberg Law.

10. Geoffrey C. Hazard et al., *The Law of Lawyering (2015); American Law Institute, Restatement of the Law (Third): The Law Governing Lawyers* (Wolters Kluwer 2000).

Chapter 13

Insurance Law Research

I. Introduction

Hartford, Connecticut, has a well-established reputation as the Insurance Capital of the United States for its large insurance companies and overall impact on the insurance industry. Insurance law practice is therefore common in Connecticut. Research related to insurance law typically involves either (1) the relationship between the insurer and insured, plus the obligations imposed through insurance policies, or (2) the regulation of the insurance industry.

II. Secondary Sources

Insurance law is well covered by treatises and practice materials. The two major national insurance treatises are *Appleman on Insurance* and *Couch on Insurance*. Each treatise covers all areas of insurance law including insurance contracts, regulations, litigation, and reinsurance. *Appleman* is available on Lexis, and *Couch* is available on Westlaw.

There are numerous treatises that cover narrow topics of insurance law such as certain types of insurance, government insurance, jurisdiction-specific insurance, insurance regulation, insurance litigation, and reinsurance. To locate an insurance law treatise, consult online insurance law research guides or search for treatises under the subject of "Insurance" on Lexis or Westlaw. *Connecticut Insurance Law* is a treatise that focuses on insurance coverage in Connecticut, including insurance contracts, policy interpretation, and agent and broker regulation.[1]

1. Michael S. Taylor, Karen L. Dowd & Brendon P. Levesque, *Connecticut Insurance Law* (3rd ed., Connecticut Law Tribune 2016).

III. Primary Law

Insurance law is primarily a matter of state law. Statutes and regulations govern the formation of insurance policies and the insurance industry. Case law has an important role in interpreting policy and contract provisions.

A. Statutes

State statutes are the major sources of law for insurance regulation, although there are federal statutes that regulate some aspects of insurance that concern issues that impact multiple states or the entire country. State insurance laws generally cover topics such as mandatory insurance coverage, uninsured motorists, no fault and personal injury insurance, the effect of cancellation or lapse of coverage, workers' compensation, and professional liability. In Connecticut, statutes related to insurance can be found in Title 38a of the *General Statutes.*

B. Regulations and Administrative Agencies

State administrative agencies regulate insurance businesses. These agencies oversee the licensing and operation of businesses that sell insurance, investigate insurance fraud, and report information related to the insurance market in the state. In Connecticut, the Department of Insurance is the agency responsible for insurance regulation. Title 38a of the *Regulations of Connecticut State Agencies* contains insurance regulations. The Department of Insurance issues bulletins that explain how it interprets laws, and it provides procedures and methods of compliance for insurers. The bulletins are available on the department's website.[2]

C. Case Law

Case law has a significant role in insurance policy interpretation and statutory interpretation. Cases related to insurance can be researched through specialized insurance law resources or through the processes described in chapter 6. For example, IRMI, a database specializing in insurance law, provides a case law library that features cases on various types of insurance, specific policy provisions, and the general insurance market. Treatises may also

---

2. Connecticut Department of Insurance Bulletins, https://portal.ct.gov/CID/Bulletins/Current-List-of-Bulletins.

be used to locate relevant case law. Some treatises provide annotations to standard insurance policies, which assists in locating case law on policy interpretation.

IV. National Association of Insurance Commissioners

The National Association of Insurance Commissioners (NAIC) is governed by the chief insurance regulators of all fifty states. The organization establishes standards and provides information and data for all state insurance regulators.

NAIC develops model laws and regulations on insurance and encourages adoption by states to achieve uniformity in insurance regulation throughout the country. *NAIC Model Laws and Regulations* provides the model laws and regulations, drafting notes, and charts that indicate the adopting states and the codification of the model laws and regulations in each state's statutes or regulations. *NAIC Model Laws and Regulations* is available on the NAIC website[3] and Lexis.

NAIC Model Laws and Regulations also references the *Proceedings of the NAIC* for each model law and regulation. *Proceedings of the NAIC* is a separate publication that records the actions of the NAIC when adopting model laws and regulations. *Proceedings of the NAIC* provides reasoning and justifications for the adopted model laws and regulations, and it is occasionally cited by courts when interpreting statutes based on the model laws.[4] The publication is available on the NAIC website,[5] Lexis, and Westlaw.

V. Insurance Policies

Some insurance companies develop their own policies, especially for specialized types of insurance, but standard insurance policies are extremely common. Standard insurance policies are created for many lines of property and casualty insurance. Insurance Services Office (ISO) is the most well-known creator of standard insurance policies. Because state insurance laws may vary, insurance policies often contain state-specific endorsements to

---

3. NAIC Model Laws and Regulations, https://content.naic.org/model-laws.
4. *Doucette v. Pomes*, 247 Conn. 442, 462 (1999).
5. NAIC Proceedings, https://content.naic.org/publications#proceedings.

comply with state-specific laws. Standard policies are periodically revised to reflect changes to the laws and insurance practices of a given state. Standard policies are numbered and dated for identification. In researching coverage related to a specific form, it is important to ensure that the correct edition is being referenced in all sources.

ISO forms cover a wide variety of lines of insurance, and they are made available through ISO and Lexis. ISO forms are numbered by the type of insurance, which is indicated by a letter code, form number, and form edition's month and year. For example, ISO Form CP 10 10 06 07 is a commercial property form, number 10 10, issued in June 2007. To research policy interpretation, a researcher should begin with secondary sources that provide explanations and analyses of policies. One major secondary source for policy interpretation is *FC&S*, which provides insurance coverage information and analyses of standard policies. *FC&S* covers property and casualty insurance, and it is available through a specialized database called *FC&S Expert Coverage Interpretation.*

Miller's Standard Insurance Policies, which is available in print and on Westlaw, provides extensive annotations to case law that interprets policy provisions for numerous personal and commercial lines of insurance. Many treatises also include annotated standard forms that address policy interpretation.

As mentioned, case law is critical to researching policy interpretation. Secondary sources on policy interpretation are the most efficient method to find relevant case law that interprets specific policy provisions.

VI. Selected Secondary Sources

There is a multitude of secondary sources that are relevant to insurance law research. However, the following secondary sources are the leading secondary sources within the area of law.

A. Treatises

Eugene R. Anderson, Jordan S. Stanzler & Lorelie S. Masters, *Insurance Coverage Litigation* (2nd ed., Aspen Publishers 2000). Available on VitalLaw.

William T. Barker, Ronald D. Kent & John Alan Appleman, *New Appleman Insurance Bad Faith Litigation* (2d ed., LexisNexis 2010). Available on Lexis.

Robert A. Bregman, Jack P. Gibson & Sean Jordan, *Professional Liability Insurance* (IRMI 2018). Available on Lexis.

Jack P. Gibson, Maureen C. McLendon, Richard J. Scislowski & W. Jeffrey Woodward, *Commercial Liability Insurance* (IRMI 2018). Available on IRMI.

Raymond A. Guenter & Elisabeth Ditomassi, *Fundamentals of Insurance Regulation* (American Bar Association 2017).

Bertram Harnett & Irving I. Lesnick, *The Law of Life and Health Insurance* (LexisNexis 1988). Available on Lexis.

David L. Leitner, Reagan W. Simpson & John M. Bjorkman, *Law and Practice of Insurance Coverage Litigation* (Thomson West 2010). Available on Westlaw.

John H. Mathias Jr., David M. Kroeger, Matthew M. Neumeier, & Jerry J. Burgdoerfer, *Directors and Officers Liability: Prevention, Insurance and Indemnification* (LexisNexis 2018). Available on Lexis.

Lee R. Russ, Thomas F. Segalla & George James Couch, *Couch on Insurance* (3rd ed., Thomson Reuters 1995). Available on Lexis.

Irvin E. Schermer & William J. Schermer, *Automobile Liability Insurance* (4th ed., Clark Boardman Callaghan 2004).

Graydon S. Staring & Dean Hansell, *Law of Reinsurance* (Clark Boardman Callaghan 2011). Available on Westlaw.

Jeffrey W. Stempel & Erik S. Knutsen, *Stempel and Knutsen on Insurance Coverage* (4th ed., Wolters Kluwer 2016). Available on VitalLaw.

Jeffrey E. Thomas & John Alan Appleman, *New Appleman on Insurance Law* (Library ed., LexisNexis 2009). Available on Lexis.

B. Policy Interpretation

Susan J. Miller & Philip Lefebvre, *Miller's Standard Insurance Policies Annotated* (Legal Research Systems, Inc. 1986). Available on Westlaw.

National Underwriter FC&S Expert Coverage Interpretation. Database available through Law.com.

C. Periodicals and Current Awareness

Best's Review

Connecticut Insurance Journal

Insurance Coverage Law Center. Database available through Law.com.

Insurance Litigation Reporter

Journal of Insurance Regulation

Journal of Risk and Insurance

About the Authors

Anne Rajotte is the Head of Research and Instruction at the University of Connecticut School of Law Library.

Jessica Rubin is a Clinical Professor of Law and Director of the Legal Practice Program and the Animal Law Clinic at the University of Connecticut School of Law.

Index